Battle Ready

Colonial Troops
1610–1774

René Chartrand · Illustrated by David Rickman

This American edition first published in 2003 by Raintree, a division of Reed
Elsevier Inc., Chicago, Illinois, by arrangement with Osprey Publishing Limited,
Oxford, England.

For information, address the publisher:
Raintree, 100 N. LaSalle, Suite 1200, Chicago, IL 60602

First published 2002
Under the title *Men-at-Arms 372: Colonial American Troops 1610–1774 (2)*
By Osprey Publishing Limited, Elms Court, Chapel Way, Botley,
Oxford, OX2 9LP
© 2002 Osprey Publishing Limited
All rights reserved.

ISBN 1-4109-0118-1

Library of Congress Cataloging-in-Publication Data is available upon request.

03 04 05 06 07   10 9 8 7 6 5 4 3 2 1

Author: René Chartrand
Illustrator: Dave Rickman
Editor: Martin Windrow
Design: Alan Hamp
Index by Alan Rutter
Originated by Grasmere Digital Imaging, Leeds, UK
Printed in China through World Print Ltd.

Abbreviations used in this text

Colonies/states: CT, Connecticut; DE, Delaware; GA, Georgia;
NC, North Carolina; NFLD, Newfoundland; NJ, New Jersey;
NH, New Hampshire; NS, Nova Scotia; NY, New York;
MA, Massachusetts; MD, Maryland; ME, Maine; PA, Pennsylvania;
RI, Rhode Island; SC, South Carolina; VA, Virginia.

Archives: BL, British Library; NAC, National Archives of Canada;
PRO, Public Records Office, Kew, UK, within which PRO/AO,
Audit Office; PRO/CO, Colonial Office; PRO/T, Treasury, & PRO/WO,
War Office.

Published sources: CSPC: *Calendar of State Papers Colonial*;
DHSNY: *Documentary History of the State of New York*; DRCHSNY:
Documents Relative to the Colonial History of the State of New York;
JSAHR: *Journal of the Society for Army Historical Research*; MC&H:
*Military Collector & Historian: Journal of the Company of Military
Historians*; PWJ: *Papers of Sir William Johnson*.

Author's Note

The history and development of the North American colonies was
most varied. Some were not initially British; some were founded by
different religious groups, while others attracted men who sought
land and riches. The evolution of their military institutions was
therefore quite varied, reflecting the fact that some were under
constant threat from American Indian, French or Spanish enemies
while others were not. Few royal troops were posted to or raised in
the colonies before the mid-18th century; consequently the
colonists had to organize their own defense if they were to survive.

Artist's Note

CONTENTS

COLONIAL TROOPS
1610–1774

MASSACHUSETTS

THE 102 "PILGRIM FATHERS" who landed at Plymouth Rock in November 1620 were religious refugees from England. The Pilgrims were fundamentalist Christians who had separated from the established church – humble people used to a hard-working life, during which they would earn their heavenly reward by their pure ways. In all that they did, they never doubted that they were carrying out the will of God. Their first years at Plymouth were difficult, but through unremitting labor and a thrifty and Spartan way of life, their colony gradually thrived. Their life was basically divided between toil and prayer.

Militia sergeant's halberd from the town of Wellesley, Massachusetts, c.1740. (Journal of the American Military Institute, 1940)

Militia
Suspicious of the nearby Indians, in 1622 the Plymouth colonists were organized into four militia companies by Miles Standish. The first meeting house in Plymouth was a sturdy affair with a flat roof upon which were mounted six cannons. Isaack de Rasiere mentioned in 1627 that, for a church service, the men "assemble by beat of the drum, each with his musket or firelock, in front of the captain's door; they have their cloaks on, and place themselves in order, three abreast, and are led by a sergeant without beat of drum. Behind him comes the governor in a long robe; beside him, on the right hand, comes the preacher with his robe on, and on the left hand the captain with his side-arms, and cloak on, and with a small cane in his hand; and so they march in good order, and each sets his arms down near him. Thus they are constantly on their guard night and day."

The early settlers of Plymouth colony had access to various types of firearms, edged weapons and armor. Corselets and helmets were in use until about the mid-1630s, but muskets alone were carried from 1643. More "trainband" companies were organized in new villages as Plymouth Bay colony expanded. In 1658 a troop of horse was organized, as well as a senior staff headed by a major. The colony suffered losses to King Philip's hostile Narraganset warriors in 1675–76. In July 1676 a "Company of Volunteers of about 200 men, English and Indian, the English not exceeding the number of 60" was raised for full-time service, to be led by Capt.Benjamin Church. This was a Ranger-type unit made up of woodsmen, which eventually trapped and killed King Philip. The colony of Plymouth Bay had remained small and, in 1691, it was amalgamated into its neighbor, the colony of Massachusetts Bay.

Massachusetts Bay
The settlement of this colony from 1628 was swift and relatively unopposed by the Indians. These settlers were "Puritans" who, like the

Miles Standish (c.1584–1656), a veteran of European campaigns, was the "captain-general" of Plymouth Colony from 1620 until his death. He never trusted the Indians and, in 1622, heard of a plot to attack the settlement by Chief Wituwamat. With eight militiamen, he trapped and killed Wituwamat and six other Indians, as shown in this 19th-century print. This murderous incident set the tone for the New Englanders' relations with Indians for decades to come.

Pilgrims, had come to America in order t practice their fundamentalist beliefs freely. From the outset, all able-bodied men in Massachuset bore arms. The first Puritan settlers brought with them 80 "bastard snaphance" muskets having four-foot barrels but no rests; ten full matchloc muskets with four-foot barrels and rests; 60 suits of pikemen's armor varnished black, and 60 pike 20 half-pikes, with a few halberds and partizan bought by the Massachusetts Bay Company. Th men were further armed with swords – ofter straight, slim-bladed thrusting weapons but als numerous broad, heavy cutlasses for slashing cut Bandoliers and belts completed the equipmen Some men had their own helmets, daggers an buff leather coats.

Clothing sent out for a hundred men at Saler in 1629 included "200 suits doublet and hose of leather" 100 suits of kersey, "100 waistcoats of green cotton, bound about with red tape," 100 "black hats lined in the brim with leather,"and 100 each of red knit caps, Monmouth caps an leather girdles, as well as shirts, shoes, an hooks-and-eyes.[1]

Militia companies were formed in the variou localities as the colony grew. The first tax levied on the inhabitants of Medford near Boston in 163 was to pay for two instructors in military tactic and, from July 1631, they drilled on the fir Friday of every month with men from th Charlestown company. The musketeers wer equipped with muskets, bandoliers with bulle bags, swords and belts, and might also wear a helmet or a hat. The pikemen had helmets, breast- and back-plates with tassets as well as pike and swords. There were usually two musketeers to every pikemar Captains and lieutenants had partizans and sergeants had halberd There were drummers, and ensigns carried the company colors. As i nearby Plymouth Colony, the English Trained Band system wa reproduced in Massachusetts. In 1630 the militiamen of Medford wer each to have a musket, a rest, a sword, a bandolier, a powder pouch wit bullets and a belt. In March 1631, the ruling authorities in Bosto further ordered that all "persons within their Towne (except magistrate and ministers) be furnished with good and sufficient armes" provided b the town if the individual could not afford them.

In October and December 1636, the companies were ordered forme into three regiments: the East, North and South regiments unde Colonels John Winthrop, John Haynes and John Endecott. Winthrop East Regiment included Boston, Roxburry, Dorchester, Weymouth an Hingham, while the two other regiments gathered companies to th

1 See *Salem 1630* (Salem, MA, 1959), pp.19–20. On arms, see Harold L.Petersen, "The Military Equipment of the Plymouth and Bay Colonies," *New England Quarterly*, XX (1947); and Harold L. Petersen & H.Charles McBarron Jr "The North Regiment, Massachusetts Bay Colony, 1636," *MC&H*, IV (1952).

north and south. An idea of what arms and equipment were required was given in John Jocelyn's 1638 recommendations for settlers who, ideally, would arrive with one "Armor compleat, light," one long musket "five foot, or five and a half near Musket bore," with a sword, a bandolier, a belt and ammunition. It was acceptable if half of the men had armor so long as all had muskets and swords. There were still many independent "Trainband" companies in outlying communities. In 1643 the militia was ordered organized into county regiments, and these units thereafter bore the names of their respective counties.

With the growth in militia units the need for specialized training increased and, during 1637, proposals were made to set up in Boston a unit to provide training for militia officers and artillery services. It was closely patterned on the City of London's "Artillery Garden" (which became the Honourable Artillery Company), which provided similar services. On March 13, 1638, Massachusetts granted a charter to "The Military Company of Massachusetts" with Capt.Robert Keayne (1595–1656) – a veteran of the London unit and one of Boston's first settlers – appointed as its first commander. Under his guidance the company became, in effect, the first military training unit and the first artillery school in the American colonies. Keayne was a proponent of volunteer military training in peacetime and a vigorous promoter of what would now be called an Officers' Training Corps. The company fulfilled this dual role and, in due course, many of Massachusetts' militia officers underwent their initial military training in its ranks. As time passed its title changed: the word "Artillery" was added in the late 1650s, "Honourable" in the early 18th century, and "Ancient" in the late 1730s, to become the Boston Ancient and Honourable Artillery Company. The company initially had buff coats (see Plate A).

Cavalry only appeared in about 1650 when horses

New England militiamen of the 1620s–30s were well armed and many also had armor, especially breast- and back-plates and helmets, as shown in this 19th-century reconstruction. There is plentiful documentary evidence for the shipment to America of essentially the full equipment of contemporary European infantry as seen on the battlefields of the Dutch and Thirty Years' Wars. (Print after A.S.Davis)

Sir Richard Saltonstall (1586–1658), a nephew of the lord mayor of London in 1597, emigrated with his family to Massachusetts in 1630, and was a founder of Watertown. He, and later his son Richard, were members of the governing council. In 1631 he returned to England owing to the illness of his two young daughters. There he helped secure the grant at the mouth of the Connecticut River which led to the settlement of Saybrook. He wears a buff coat of superior quality trimmed with gold buttons, and a gold-laced sword belt. (Print after portrait)

were becoming common in the colony. It wa casually related in Johnson's rather religiou *Wonders Working Providence* that there was "of lat a very gallant horse-troop" who were actuall members of "the foot companies turned Trooper (when their own Regiment is not in exercise) fo the encouragement of others." The trend too on, and by 1663 Massachusetts required tha cavalrymen were to furnish their own horse, arm and equipment in order to be admitted to a troo – a number of other conditions governed th commissioning of such troops. Four years lat the cavalry numbered 12 troops of 160 trooper each. In April 1675 they were reported to be we equipped, wearing "buff coats, pistols, hanger and corselets" (CSPC 1675). These mounte militiamen proved to be very useful durin King Philip's War (see Plate B).

In 1667, the Massachusetts militia strength wa estimated at "30,000 fighting men" between 16 an 60 years of age, who trained eight times in th year; each town also had artillerymen who traine weekly. Nine years later it was estimated tha between 30,000 and 40,000 able-bodied me could be mobilized, including 4,000 in Bosto The trained bands numbered 6,000 of the bes equipped infantry, which now had "no pikemen. Most of the bands and troops of horse were in th Boston area, as were the main fortifications although there was also a small fort at Marblehea – said to be "of little use" (CSPC 1667). In lat 1675, when King Philip's Narragansets and thei allies struck in countless places, some 700 infantry and 200 horseme were mobilized in Massachusetts and Plymouth Bay. With Connecticu militiamen and allied Indians, they prevailed against the hostile Indian at the bloody Great Swamp Fight of December 19.

In 1676 the Boston Militia Regiment, still divided into only fou overgrown companies, was doubled to eight companies. By this time th frontier had advanced farther to the west, and the unit had become a cit regiment in much the same way as town militia regiments in England. was probably adequate to face a moderate attack from a seaborn European enemy, but much less suited to fighting King Philip's Indians

In the following decades the militia continued to expand as th province grew and more county regiments were added. In the early day of the colony training was held once a week, then once a month fro 1631, decreasing to eight days a year in 1637, six days from 1660, an four days from 1693. By then regimental musters were held only onc every three years (except for Boston).

Officers were usually chosen by the men of their companies and thei names submitted to the legislative "General Assembly" for approval. A able-bodied men liable to militia service were to have arms and ammunitio when appearing for drills. By the 1693 Militia Act, these consisted of musket, a cartouch box, and a sword or (from 1734) cutlass. Sergeants carried halberds. The county militia regiments formed the pool of men from which temporary units were raised for expeditions from the late 17th century. In time these became "provincial" troops in the 1740s, serving during most of a year (see below). In 1744 some 150 "grenadiers" chosen from the tallest men were formed in the York County Regiment and instructed "in the Exercise of throwing hand Granadoes."

Such troops were called up for active service in emergencies, such as in early August 1757 following the fall of Fort William Henry, when Governor Thomas Pownall ordered western Massachusetts to provide a quarter of the men from each of the province's regiments except for Maine, Nantucket and Duke's County. The long years of war, which began in the 1740s, also produced a more efficient local militia. In Marblehead, for instance, the two companies were reportedly badly clothed and "trained to no military discipline" in 1714. By 1766 the town's militia had grown to a seven-company regiment which was "well clad," with good men who were well trained in "the use of their arms, and the various motions and marches." Few seem to have had uniforms outside of Boston, but this may have changed somewhat in the 1760s or early 1770s. At Bunker Hill in 1775, Capt.John Chester recalled that his company "marched, with our frocks and trowsers on over our clothes, (for our company is in uniform wholly blue, turned up with red,) for we were loath to expose ourselves by our dress" (*Historical Magazine*, XIII).

Independent volunteer militia units

In the mid-18th century, besides the Boston Militia Regiment which gathered all able-bodied men, the city's militia had a number of distinct units made up of the wealthier gentlemen volunteers. As already mentioned, the Ancient and Honourable Artillery Company, raised in 1638, had first acted as a combination training school and artillery company. By the mid-18th century it had become more of a wealthy merchants' company, its members often also being members of the Boston Militia Regiment. Another militia "Train of Artillery" unit of volunteer gunners was then raised to serve the guns in Boston, and

Map of the localities involved in King Philip's War of 1675–76.

King Philip's Narraganset and other Indians carried out numerous attacks on New England settlements in 1675. At Brookfield, Massachusetts, they tried setting fire to the blockhouse defending the village with a blazing barrel made into a "cart." The attempt failed there, but Brookfield, like many other towns, was evacuated. Other localities fell to these attacks, and up to 1,000 settlers were killed – ten percent of the adult male population.

attached to the Boston Militia Regiment. This regiment also had an elite grenadier company.

The Boston Cadet Company appeared in 1728 when its first recorded function – providing an escort for Governor Burnet – took place on July 4. This was mainly a ceremonial unit; it was presented with a color on May 26, 1729, and went on to escort governors and generals on solemn or festive occasions, such as Governor William Shirley's entry into Boston on July 18, 1745 following the surrender of Louisbourg. Its early dress is unknown but there is much information from 1772 (see Plate H). Just before the Revolution the town of Great Barrington also had its own Independent Company of Cadets.

In 1754, a cavalry company to provide a mounted escort to the governor was formed among the young gentlemen of Boston. This Company of Horse Guards existed until the Revolution.

The students of Harvard College (now University) were exempted from military duty; however, in about 1772 a "military company" was formed among the student volunteers. As they were nearly all opposed to British policy in the colonies, the governor delayed signing an order that arms be delivered to the company – "But these young men were not discouraged, for they procured wooden guns to exercise with, and were reviewed using them" by members of the legislature. The company was disbanded at the Revolution but later reraised.

The preserved door of the Sheldon house at Deerfield, Massachusetts, bearing the marks and holes of tomahawk blows made during an attack by French and Indians on February 29, 1704.

Massachusetts Provincials

Early on, some officers and men of the militia were called for active duty, as the colony had to provide its armed forces at its own expense. Massachusetts colonial laws specified that militiamen could be drafted to serve full time. Boston had an elaborate paid watch of men drawn from the various militia companies who served in turns; in 1679 it numbered some 70 officers and men. The commander of the watch carried a half-pike, the sergeants had halberds and the men muskets. Forts were also garrisoned by embodied militiamen. Castle William in Boston harbor had a commander who was also the chief gunner with responsibility for the upkeep of its many cannon.

Forts on the frontier were garrisoned by local militiamen serving their turns on watch – not an ideal system, but the only affordable solution. For garrisoning an isolated fort, militiamen in Massachusetts would be "impressed" if enough volunteers were not found, all to be "well Armed with fixed fire-lock arms – one pound of powder [and] three pounds of shot" per man, such as the 20 drafted in August 1680 to serve at the fort built at Casco Bay in Maine (Sewall's Diary).

In April 1690 a "Foot Regiment" was raised especially for Sir William Phips' successful expedition by sea against the French in Acadia. The regiment had seven companies totaling 446 officers and men and was

Captured New England colonists being taken to Canada by Indians allied to the French. Most were taken in Massachusetts and ransomed by the French; some were adopted into Indian families; while others might be even less fortunate, and the accounts of survivors were harrowing. This being said, many survived because the French paid the Indians far more money for live prisoners than for scalps. The New Englanders, by contrast, paid handsomely for scalps, so that their allied Indians usually slaughtered the French settlers rather than make them prisoners.

led by Maj.William Johnson. Port Royal surrendered without a fight in May, was plundered and then abandoned; Johnson's men were back home by June. This quick triumph seemed to show the way to beat the French and Indians; rather excessively encouraged, Phips decided to attack Quebec by sea! A colonial army was quickly raised, consisting of about 2,300 men divided into seven battalions, each bearing the name of its major commanding: Quincy, Phillips, Hutchinson, Henchman, Appleton, Gedney and Saltonstall. Most were from Massachusetts, but there were a few companies from the colonies of New York and Plymouth Bay. Arriving before Quebec in mid-October, the Massachusetts fleet was greeted by the fiery Count Frontenac's answer to their summons "by the muzzle of my cannons" and, in the ensuing battles, the provincials were totally defeated (see Plate C).

Many smaller parties were mobilized for short periods on the frontiers over the following years (some with snowshoes, in the winter of 1703–04). In July 1704 more than 500 Bostonians mounted an attack on the French at Port Royal, but without success. In May 1707 a second attack was launched by two Massachusetts regiments raised for the purpose, Wainright's "of the red" and Hilton's "of the blue." This expedition, too, was repulsed. In September 1710 two regiments from Massachusetts participated in the capture of Port Royal. In 1711, Vetch's and Walton's regiments were part of Admiral Walker's abortive attempt on Quebec. From 1720, Col.Walton with 200 men later followed by other

Musket of the reign of Queen Anne (first decade of the 18th century), made by Brush in London and restocked in New England. Note the "dog lock," the notch and safety catch to hold the cock back. (*Antiques*, June 1927)

9

Castle William at the entrance of Boston harbor saluted by a British warship, c.1729. Begun in 1634 and built at the expense of Massachusetts colony, the first fort made of wood and earth was destroyed by fire in 1673. A larger "castle" with stone bastions mounting 38 cannon replaced it and, in the 1690s, was up-graded to hold 54 guns. This was considerably enlarged between 1701 and 1703 to a major fort mounting 100 guns – this is the fort shown at left in this print. Yet another expansion in 1740 added the Shirley Bastion which boasted an additional 20 guns of 42-pound caliber, making it the most powerful coastal fort in the British North American colonies. Garrisoned by Massachusetts troops until the 1760s, it was then used by the British Army, which destroyed it when Boston was evacuated in March 1776.

troops campaigned against the Indians in Maine, until they came to term in late 1725. In January 1743 two artillery companies of 60 men each wer mobilized from the Dorchester Militia to serve the "Great Artillery" ii Castle William in Boston. These were said by Governor Shirley to be th first units solely devoted to artillery raised in the colony. Three 50-stron; companies of "Snowshoe Men" were raised from November 30, 1743 t protect the frontier until apparently replaced by Stoddard's Regiment i 1744 (Governor Shirley wanted to raise ten companies, but it seems tha only three were actually formed).[2] They were equipped with musket; tomahawks, moccasins and showshoes, but probably could do littl against the many Indian and Canadian war parties, who were expel woodsmen.

It was in the more conventional aspects of European-style warfare tha New Englanders achieved their first spectacular success. In 1745, whil Bowen's and Willis' regiments were embodied to guard the frontier, a artillery corps and seven other infantry regiments (Pepperell's 1s Waldo's 2nd, Moulton's 3rd, Willard's 4th, Hale's 5th, Richmond's 6t and Goreham's 7th) were raised from February for the expeditio against Louisbourg (NS). All gave excellent service during the siege however, instead of being sent home after the surrender of the Frencl garrison in July, many men were kept in garrison there until April 174€ In late July a "Company of Artificers and Workmen" was formed fron the men in the regiments at Louisbourg so that the necessary repair would be "better forwarded." The era of relatively short service fo

2 *Correspondence of William Shirley*, I, p.138.

specific expeditions had ended, and that of longer "provincial" service was beginning.

Two provincial regiments were raised from June 1746, one of ten companies and one of 17 companies of 100 men each, to serve until October 31, 1747. Some 440 men were later posted to the frontier, joined by over 200 more from June 1746. (These included a 50-man company with dogs, so as to provide warning of approaching enemies; they seem to have been of little use, as the dogs were disposed of in November 1746.) Dwight's Regiment was deployed at Deerfield and other areas in western Massachusetts until 1748. About 500 provincials were in Grand Pré (NS) when Col.Noble and many of his men were killed by a daring French and Indian raid on January 31, 1747. Six companies of 70 men each were later retained for service at Annapolis Royal (NS) until February 24, 1748. These units did not have uniforms, but some men might get clothing while on service. Four of the 38 men of Pomeroy's company, Dwight's Regiment, were issued coats; five received breeches and waistcoats and four got "caps," while the rest would have enlisted wearing their own clothes.

Sir William Pepperell (1696–1759) in 1747. Colonel of the Maine militia in 1726, successful in business, wealthy, honest in politics, shrewd, cool-tempered in crisis, and very popular, Pepperell was made major-general of provincial troops in 1745 to lead the attack on Fortress Louisbourg – a task which was brilliantly performed. He was later made colonel of regular army regiments, named lieutenant-general in the regular army, and created baronet in the year of his death – the only American colonist to be elevated to the nobility. Pepperell had a full-length portrait by John Smibert made in 1747, in which he wears an all-scarlet costume with gold buttons and gold lace edging the waistcoat and hat. The same artist also painted this half-length portrait of better quality; here Pepperell wears an all-blue coat, a scarlet waistcoat, gold lace and buttons, with a command baton held in the right hand. (Print after Smibert)

The Seven Years' War

In 1754, Governor Shirley appointed Lt.Col.John Winslow to lead some 800 militiamen against the French in the Kennebec River area in Maine; the expedition that late summer failed to find the enemy. From February 10, 1755, Shirley raised the "New England Regiment" of which he was colonel; paid for by the British crown, it was to serve as a provincial unit recruited mostly in Massachusetts. Lieutenant-Colonel Winslow led the first battalion, Lt.Col.Scott the second. Shirley's Regiment was sent to Nova Scotia and deployed against the French with Col.Monckton's British regulars in the short campaign that secured Fort Beauséjour and Gaspareau. This was the first time that New England troops had served alongside a sizeable force of British regulars, and the arrogant attitude of many British officers was keenly felt. One British officer, Lt.William Jacobs, felt that "the unkind behavior of the regulars to the irregulars" was so excessive that resentment had run very high. The Massachusetts officers were "men of fortune in New England" who had "left their estates to serve their King and Country," and their troops were "all volunteers." Jacobs believed that "the New England troop" would not want to serve with regulars again – a great loss, as "the Americans are a brave [and] honest people" (BL, Add. Ms 4164).

The men of both battalions were issued coats, breeches, shirts, neck cloths, waistcoats, stockings and shoes, and "caps" are listed rather than hats. They also had blankets, haversacks, accoutrements including cartridge boxes and belts and some also had powder horns. They were armed with muskets from the royal stores. Captain Abijah Willard noted on April 9, 1755 that "their clothes tho [were already] mean and [of] scandalous" quality when issued in Boston. The color of the uniforms of

Winslow's 1st Battalion is mentioned as "the Ble⬛ battalion" by Willard on August 6; this seems t⬛ imply that Scott's 2nd Battalion had uniforms ⬛ another color. In February 1756, Scott's battalio⬛ was still posted at Fort Cumberland (former⬛ Beauséjour) and its worn-out clothing was bein⬛ replaced by waistcoats made from capture⬛ French cloth, pairs of Indian stockings and India⬛ shoes.[3]

From March 1755 Massachusetts raised an⬛ paid for three other regiments of 500 men each ⬛ Willard's, William's and Titcomb's (Bagley's fror⬛ September). Sent to Lake George (NY) in Jul⬛ they were part of Major-General William Johnson⬛ army which defeated the French attack i⬛ September. Among their supplies were cartridg⬛ boxes, powder flasks, powder horns, knapsack⬛ bullet pouches, hatchets, "small arms" (includin⬛ ten for field officers), drums, and a color for eac⬛ regiment. Also raised from April 28, 1755 was ⬛ small "Train of Artillery" led by an engineer a⬛ captain, one artillery lieutenant, with an assistan⬛ and three sub-engineers and 16 gunners. I⬛ had two 32-pounders, six 18-pounders, tw⬛ 12-pounders and a mortar (PWJ, I) – such a⬛ impressive battery of ordnance must obviousl⬛ have required many more attached infantrymer⬛ as laborers. One regiment, according t⬛ Parkman, had a blue uniform faced with red⬛ A thousand extra pairs of red breeches wer⬛ ordered in August. The lost clothing an⬛ equipment reported in Capt.Ingersol's Company⬛ William's Regiment, at the battle of Lake Georg⬛

ABOVE **Colonel Samuel Waldo (1695–1759), a wealthy merchant, raised a Massachusetts regiment in 1745 and led it most competently during the siege of Fortress Louisbourg He was later promoted brigadier-general. Here he wears a brown coat and breeches, red waistcoat, gold buttons and lace. (Print after a 1747 portrait by John Smibert)**

LEFT **Sir William Shirley (1693–1771) was born in England and emigrated in 1731 to Massachusetts, where he was very successful in business and politics, becoming its governor in 1741–45 and 1753–57. Shirley was one of the most influential leaders advocating the conquest of New France. He was commander-in-chief in 1755–56 following Gen.Braddock's death, until Lord Loudoun's arrival in North America. Colonel of British royal regiments in 1746 and 1754, lieutenant-general and knighted in 1759, governor of the Bahamas 1761–69, Shirley retired in his beloved Massachusetts in 1770. (Print after T.Hudson)**

---

3 Shirley's New England Regiment raised under the authority of Massachusetts Bay Colony should not be confused with Shirley's 51st Regiment of Foot, a regular British Army unit raised in North America, of which he was also colonel.

n September 8 included two coats, two waistcoats, two hats, two caps, 12 blankets and five hatchets. On September 9, Gridley's Regiment was also raised and served during the fall.

In February, March and April 1756, Massachusetts authorized 3,500 infantrymen in regiments (Bagley's, Dwight's, Gridley's, Plaisted's, Ruggle's and Tacher's) of 500 men each. Two companies of artillery totaling 221 officers and men were also raised and attached to Gridley's Regiment. All were posted in garrisons in the area of Lake George. The men were to have blue coats, red or blue breeches, hats, canteens, knapsacks, blankets and powder horns. A deserter from Bagley's wore a blue coat and a red waistcoat in May.

From February 7, 1757, Massachusetts authorized only one large regiment of 1,800 men divided into 17 companies under Col.Joseph Frye. They were posted mostly at Fort Edward and at Fort William Henry, where some 800 men were lost to Montcalm's French and Indians in early August. Part of the militia was called out, and a train of artillery – to have eight guns – was organized from August 8.

In 1758 Massachusetts greatly increased its war effort, authorizing even regiments of 1,000 men each to be raised from March 2. Ruggle's, Bagley's, Prebble's, Joseph William's, Partridge's and Doty's were with Abercromby's army in the failed July attack against Ticonderoga. Colonel Bradstreet's successful expedition against Fort Frontenac in August included 432 men from William's and 248 from Doty's regiments.

From February 28, 1759, some 6,800 men were to be raised of which 400 were to be divided into four companies to garrison Fort Penobscot, the remainder divided into regiments. These were Prebble's, William William's, Joseph William's, Doty's and Nichol's, posted in various garrisons in New York; Bagley's was in Louisbourg, while Ruggle's and Willard's served with Amherst's army which at last occupied Ticonderoga and Crown Point. Up to 400 more were sent to Fort Cumberland on the Nova Scotia frontier. In addition to these troops, some 300 pioneers

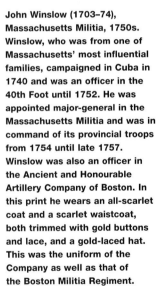

John Winslow (1703–74), Massachusetts Militia, 1750s. Winslow, who was from one of Massachusetts' most influential families, campaigned in Cuba in 1740 and was an officer in the 40th Foot until 1752. He was appointed major-general in the Massachusetts Militia and was in command of its provincial troops from 1754 until late 1757. Winslow was also an officer in the Ancient and Honourable Artillery Company of Boston. In this print he wears an all-scarlet coat and a scarlet waistcoat, both trimmed with gold buttons and lace, and a gold-laced hat. This was the uniform of the Company as well as that of the Boston Militia Regiment.

Fort Western was built in 1754 by Massachusetts troops under John Winslow on the site of present-day Augusta, Maine, along with Fort Halifax (Winslow, Maine), to protect the northern frontier against Indian war parties. This late 19th-century print is a conjectural view of its probable appearance.

Colonel Jacob Fowle (1704–78), Massachusetts Militia, c.1760. Fowle was listed in the Boston Militia Regiment as late as 1773. All-scarlet coat including lining, scarlet waistcoat and breeches, gold lace and buttons, crimson sash, gold sword hilt, gold-laced hat with red plume. (Print after J.S.Copley)

raised in the colony were with Wolfe's army durin the siege of Quebec.

Some 5,000 men divided into five regimen were authorized raised in 1760. Ruggle's, Willard and Thomas' were with Haviland's army, Bagley was in Louisbourg, and Thwing's remained i garrisons. From April 4, 1761, three regimen (Thwing's, Hoar's and Saltonstall's) totaling 3,00 men were raised, two serving at Crown Poir and one at Halifax. Some 3,200 men in thre regiments were raised from March and April 176 for the same garrisons; Hoar's, at Halifax, too part in the recapture of St. John's (NFLD) from th French in September. Some 268 men wer authorized for winter service at Halifax and 323 fo western outposts, serving until the spring of 176.

There was also a company of 50 men on guar at Castle William in Boston from Decembe 1757, raised to 60 from June 1762. The unifor was probably as for other provincial troops; deserter from Castle William had on "an old Blu Coat" in July 1761. Massachusetts also ha Rangers, "battoemen" (boatmen) and othe support personnel which, in 1758 alone, totaled another 3,000 men.

The colony's contribution to British victory was substantial: about third of its able-bodied men served during the war, and high taxatio drove some to bankruptcy.[4]

NEW HAMPSHIRE

Militia

The first settlements were established in 1623 in the Piscataqua Rive area, and consisted mostly of fishermen; but some "plantations"wit small forts had been built by the early 1630s. A "soldier"was sent in 163 to organize a militia and train the settlers, who already faced threa from pirates and suspicious Indians. In 1632, 20 armed men fror Boston were joined on small vessels by 40 more from Piscataqua (Dove Neck, NH) to chase the pirate Dixie Bull. The colonists were well armec a 1635 inventory reveals that they had "3 sackers, 3 minions, 2 falcon 2 rabenets, 4 murtherers, 2 chambers, 22 arquebuses, 4 muskets, 4 fowling pieces, 67 carbines, 6 pairs of pistols, 61 swords and belts, 1 halberds, 31 head-pieces [helmets], 82 beaver spears, 50 flasks, – pairs o bandoliers" with ammunition, and "2 drums, 15 recorders and hautbois.

From 1641 the settlements on the Piscataqua River passed under th jurisdiction of Massachusetts, and their men formed part of its militi until New Hampshire Colony was separated from Massachusetts an created independently by royal order in 1679, this order being receive at Portsmouth, New Hampshire, in January 1680. On March 16 th

---

4 Figures in the *Massachusetts Acts and Resolves* are sometimes confusing, and Fred Anderson's calculations in his *A People's Army* are accepted as the most reliable. Data on small independent units and Rangers is scarcer, a sometimes these are not specified in the legislation.

rganization of a militia was ordered; this initially
ad an infantry company for each town of
ortsmouth, Dover, Exeter and Hampton, with an
rtillery company and Capt.Mason's troop of
orse at Portsmouth, the capital. The troop of
orse was disbanded a few years later. More
ompanies were organized as the colony grew
nd, in 1689, these were collectively termed the
Jew Hampshire Regiment of Militia.

The approximately 750 New Hampshire
nilitiamen were often engaged against raiding
ndians, especially from 1689, with some few
erving periods of time as garrisons in outlying
ontier forts. Indian raids continued in the early
700s, often against isolated houses – like the eight
ettlers killed in their dwelling at Oyster River in
706. Parties of militiamen were constantly out
couting on the frontier. There were many Indian
aids in 1711 and much skirmishing took place,
ith about half of the men in the colony on
hort-term service guarding the frontier. The
ndian raids continued until July 1713, when a
eace treaty was agreed.

Detailed militia laws were passed in 1718–19,
pecifying regiments made up of every able-bodied
nan from 16 to 60 years of age. Hostilities with the
ndians resumed in 1722 and some militiamen
vere mobilized into scouting parties for short
eriods of time. In 1725 the Indians were finally

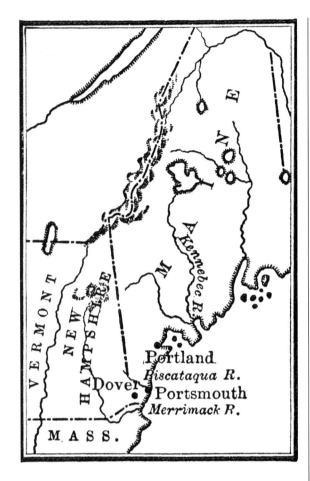

ubdued, largely thanks to reinforcements from Massachusetts. By 1730,
nilitia strength was estimated at about 1,800 men divided into two reg-
ments, though these were reported "destitute of proper arms" nine years
ater. Governor Benning Wentworth took steps to improve the militia in
he early 1740s and, in 1744, he mobilized some 40 to 50 militiamen to
cout the frontier. A year later scouts were again on duty on the frontier,
ncluding 15 mounted men under the command of Capt.Nathaniel
Drake. In 1746 more scouts were enlisted for the usual short periods
about a month at a time), and there were some skirmishes with Indians.
Robert Rogers, later to become famous as a Ranger officer, was a private
n Daniel Ladd's scouting company that year. These scouts were not
Rangers but were expected to give some warning and protection.
cattered in various frontier communities, they numbered 174 men by
he end of "King George's War" in 1748. Despite the ostensible return of
eace a troop of horse was raised in Kingston during 1750.

The New Hampshire militia was reported to be in poor shape at the
outset of the Seven Years' War. There was "hardly a Regiment of the
Militia in the Province" that had a pound of powder per man. Its
nilitiamen were "provided with arms but in general of the meanest sort,"
nd it was "not in the power of the people to procure good arms"
PRO/WO 34/101). Yet the province had passed a new militia act in 1754
vhich stipulated training four times per year, and provided for the
mbodiment of militiamen for watch duty or into provincial service. The

Map of colonial New Hampshire
and Maine. The district or
province of Maine was part of
Massachusetts until it became a
state in 1820. Settled from 1623
along the Piscataqua River, it
was the area most exposed to
Indian attacks. By 1671 its militia
amounted to 700 men divided
into companies. These were
gathered into the Yorkshire
Regiment until 1739–40, when
it was split into the Eastern
Regiment, mustering 1,300 men,
and the Western Regiment with
1,500. Most Maine militiamen
were foot soldiers but there was
a troop of horse at Kittery from
the 1720s.

Militia sergeant's halberd from Portsmouth, New Hampshire, c.1720. (*Journal of the American Military Institute*, 1940)

Militia sergeant's halberd from Portsmouth, New Hampshire, c.1720. (*Journal of the American Military Institute*, 1940)

Fort No.4 on the Connecticut River, in a remarkable reconstruction built in the 1980s. The fort was built by Massachusetts settlers in 1743–44 at the fourth and most exposed of the land grants, hence its unusual name. Captain Phineas Stevens and 30 Massachusetts militiamen resisted a two-day siege by the French and Indians on April 7–9, 1747. The area was transferred from Massachusetts to New Hampshire in 1753; this made little difference to the French and Indians, and its New Hampshire militia garrison repulsed continuing raids in 1754 and 1757. (Photo: RC)

war obviously improved the situation. The colonists' military spirit was high; New Hampshire contributed the highest number of men to provincial service proportionate to its population, and its militia was totally reorganized. In 1760 the colony's militia amounted to nine regiments of infantry and one regiment of cavalry, named "Horse Guards." The last royal governor, John Wentworth, decided to augment the number of regiments in late 1773 when the 10th, 11th and 12th regiments were organized. By 1775 there was also a Company of Cadets.

There seems to be very little evidence for uniforms being worn by the New Hampshire militia until a few years before the American Revolution. These were then red with different facings, as the 11th Regiment had sky blue (see Plate H). The officers of an unidentified unit had scarlet faced with dark blue collar, cuffs and lapels, gold buttons and lace at the buttonholes, white waistcoat and red breeches, according to an officer's portrait; he may have belonged to the 2nd Regiment, but there is no certainty of this.

New Hampshire Provincials

As described above, small detachments of militiamen were often embodied for guard duty on the colony's extensive frontiers. A couple of New Hampshire companies also participated in the ill-fated 1707 expedition against Port Royal. In 1711, 100 men were also contributed to Admiral Walker's failed expedition to Quebec. In 1745 New Hampshire contributed 500 men to the Louisbourg expedition: 350 organized in a seven-company regiment under Col.Samuel Moore, and the remainder attached to a Massachusetts regiment. In June 1746 New Hampshire raised one regiment of nine companies of 100 men each, which was discharged on October 31, 1747.

From June 1754, French and Indian raids on the frontier caused detachments from the militia to be embodied in provincial service. Captain John Webster's company served from June 14 to July 24; three more detachments under Majors Goffe and Bellow and Col.Willard were on duty at Fort No.4, Fort Dummer, Walpole and Keene from August to November 1754.

On April 11, 1755 the province approved the raising of a 500-man regiment to be in service for six months under Col.Joseph Blanchard. The unit built Fort Edward near Lake George (NY) during August and September, and fought at the battle of Lake George. On September 5 another 300-man regiment under Col.Peter Gillman was raised as

View of the interior of Fort No.4 as it might have appeared in the 1740s–50s. As can be seen, the houses of the settlement's inhabitants were clustered together to form a fort, the outside walls being sturdy and pierced with loopholes. Small pieces of ordnance could be mounted on the second stories of the corner buildings. This type of fort-settlement was not exceptional and could also be found on the frontiers of Pennsylvania and Virginia. (Photo: RC)

The outside log picket line at Fort No.4. This would be the first line of defense which would slow down attackers before they reached the fort's walls, giving time for the militiamen to get to their posts within. The Connecticut River is in the background. (Photo: RC)

reinforcements. A company of 91 men under Capt.Robert Rogers wa[s] kept in service at Forts William Henry and Edward with troops fro[m] other colonies during the winter of 1755–56; Rogers' company was real[ly] a Ranger unit.

On April 1, 1756, a 500-man regiment under Col.Nathaniel Meser[ve] was raised to join another abortive expedition to Crown Point. O[n] February 25, 1757 a regiment of 350 men was raised, again und[er] Col.Meserve, part being sent to Halifax (NS) and 200 to Fort Willia[m] Henry, which fell to the French on August 3; some 80 men were lost i[n] the siege and the ensuing massacre by the Indians. An outraged colon[y] immediately raised (from August 17) a 250-man battalion of two caval[ry] and three infantry companies under Maj.Robert Tash, which served a[t] Fort No.4 until November.

Colonel John Hart's New Hampshire Regiment was authorized t[o] serve for nine months on March 24, 1758, and 610 of all ranks were pa[rt] of Gen.Abercromby's army – but not deployed at Ticonderoga – o[n] July 8. On March 7, 1759 a regiment of 700 men under Col.Zacche[us] Lovewell was raised and sent to Oswego. On March 1, 1760 a regime[nt] of 800 men under Col.John Goffe was raised; and in April 1761 an[d] 1762 a regiment of 534 officers and men was authorized for both year[s]. These were mostly posted at Crown Point, at Fort No.4 and other pos[ts] in that area.

New Hampshire provincials had no uniforms; they reported for servi[ce] wearing their own clothes, and seemingly often carrying their own ar[ms] unless issued with military weapons and accoutrements by the Crow[n]. The variety could be impressive. A 1757 inventory of the belongings [of] Maj.John Gillman included a newly made blue coat and blue breeches, [a] coat of "Fine Duroy," another of light colored cloth, a scarlet "jacket[,"] another of velvet and a green one with silver lace, buckskin breeches, [a] gold-laced hat, a drab greatcoat and a silver-hilted sword.

CONNECTICUT

Militia

Some 250 colonists from Massachusetts settled on the west bank of th[e] Connecticut River in early 1636. No militia was formed initially, b[ut] relations with the Pequot Indians became tense and the settlers we[re] ordered to assemble and drill once a month. On April 23, 1637 th[e] Pequots struck at Wethersfield; and on May 1, representatives from fi[ve] towns voted to raise a force of 90 men to serve for a month against th[e] Pequots. John Mason, a veteran of campaigns in the Netherlands, was [its] captain. The alliance of the Mohicans, the Pequots' traditional enemie[s,] was eagerly accepted. On May 23 the Pequots' main fortified town nea[r] Mystic (CT) was attacked and taken by Mason's men. Nearly all th[e] Pequot men, women and children were killed as a stunning victo[ry] turned into a bloodbath. The 90 Connecticut militiamen were we[ll] armed with swords and muskets and equipped with armor (see Plate A[).]

Following the Pequot War, the assembly decreed that "every one th[at] beares armes shall be compleatly furnished with armes (viz), a musket[,] a sworde, bandaleers, a rest," and with ammunition. Inventories [of] belongings of the early 1640s reveal that the early settlers were general[ly]

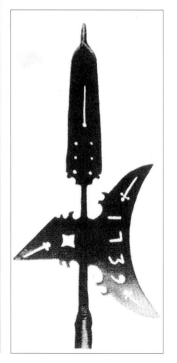

Militia sergeant's halberd from the town of Guilford, Connecticut, dated 1739. (*Journal of the American Military Institute*, 1940)

·ll armed, with swords, muskets and bandoliers; one John Olmstead ·so had a pike, a corselet and two pistols. The Indian menace to the ·tlers had largely subsided and militia training was somewhat lax for ·me years, until Britain's wars with Holland brought tensions with ·ighboring New Netherlands from the mid-1650s onwards. The militia ·en had about 800 men, and a troop of horse was raised in Hartford in ·58, but there were no major clashes with the Dutch.

The **New Haven Colony** had also been established by Puritan settlers · an independent entity in 1638. Its militia in 1642 had 217 men divided ·to four company-like "squadrons." Each man furnished his own

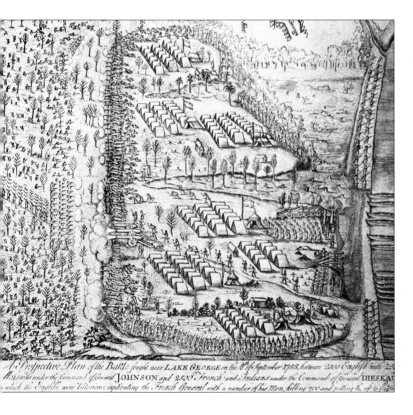

The battle of Lake George, September 8, 1755. This print by Samuel Blodget, a sutler with the Massachusetts troops present at the battle, gives a lively sense of the disposition of the troops – the New Englanders in the large enclosed camp against the lake shore, and their attackers advancing through the forest on the left. The Canadians and Indians advocated hit-and-run tactics, but the French General Dieskau decided on a European-style attack with his freshly landed regulars. The well-entrenched New England troops beat off the French and captured the wounded Dieskau. Sir William Johnson, commanding the New Englanders, was also wounded, but the Connecticut Col.Phineas Lyman, commander of the colony's 1st Provincial Regiment, successfully took over command and the enemy withdrew.

19

weapons, but pikes were provided by the colony's government. Artillerymen were added in New Haven in 1645. By 1656 there were also mounted militiamen at New Haven, Milford, Stamford, Guilford and Branford. Surprisingly, pikemen were still common as late as 1663, at least in the New Haven company. New Haven Colony and its militia were integrated into Connecticut in 1665.

With the recapture of New York by the Dutch in 1673, Connecticut's leaders ordered some 500 militiamen – a third of the total strength – to be mounted to patrol the coast: in effect, they were to become dragoons. It was a radical measure that would define Connecticut's defense policy for over 80 years. The fact that it could be ordered at all reveals that the wealth of the colony had greatly increased.

Two years later King Philip of the Narragansets launched a series of Indian attacks that shook New England, although Connecticut was less affected than other colonies. Patrols were made between some towns. In November 1675, Connecticut contributed 315 men to the New England force. From May to October 1676 some 350 militia dragoons were kept on duty against the Indians; the men brought their own horses, arms, equipment and clothes, but could be compensated for the loss of their property.

Colonel David Wooster, Connecticut Militia, c.1770. Wooster was a colonel of Connecticut provincial regimen until 1762 and was active in th Seven Years' War, but the uniform shown is of a somewha later style, with an epaulette. (Anne S.K.Brown Military Collection, Brown University)

Connecticut militiamen were embodied, sometimes by draft, during the wars with the French and Indians. It seems that as late as the 1680s some Connecticut militiamen favored protective quilted clothing, according to Governor Andros. In 1690 some 200 men went to Albany, and three years later 150 dragoons were again detached there. During 1704–09 up to 800 militiamen patrolled the frontier, mostly on horseback in summer and on snowshoes in winter.

Years of peace followed, but in 1724 an Indian threat led to the Hartford Dragoons being mobilized and sent for seven weeks to western Massachusetts; a few dozen militiamen were also put on guard in frontier towns. Several attempts were made to reorganize the militia in the 1720s and 1730s, but to no avail, although the proportion of mounted men acting as dragoons appears to have considerably decreased with more emphasis being given to foot troops.

The advent of war with Spain in 1739 changed attitudes and Connecticut became more militant. In October 1739, 'ten good cannons' were added to the coastal battery at New London and, more fundamentally, the whole militia was reorganized into 13 numbered regiments. For instance, the 1st Regiment gathered the companies of Hartford, Windsor, Symsbury, Bolton, Tolland, Harwinton, Torrington, New Hartford, Barkhemstead, Hartland, Colebrook, Winchester and Farmington; the 2nd Regiment, those of New Haven, Milford, Brandford and Derby; the 3rd Regiment, those of New London, Norwich, Lyme, and so forth. Each regiment was encouraged to form a

troop of horse if none existed; and some were very receptive to this appeal, the Lebanon town militiamen in the 12th Regiment having two troops by 1741.

The May 1741 Militia Act further specified that men from 15 to 50 years of age were to be enlisted; companies of foot or horse would have 64 officers and men, who would provide themselves with the usual arms, accoutrements and equipment. Fines would go to the purchase of colors, halberds, drums and trumpets. There seem to have been few gunners, but in the 1740s and probably earlier there was an artillery company made up of students at Yale College in New Haven, called the "College Artillery."

According to the March 1758 Militia Act, officers and men were to "fully equip themselves" and have "one good knapsack and blanket" if called to duty. No uniforms appear to have been worn by Connecticut militiamen until the 1750s and then only by specialized units – e.g. the troop of cavalry of the 11th Militia Regiment had blue coats in 1758, and the New London Artillery had blue faced with buff in 1762 (see Plate H). The Governor's Foot Guard company raised in 1769 were clothed in red coats faced with black and trimmed with yellow lace, buff waistcoat and breeches and grenadier caps. A second company of the Governor's Foot Guard raised in 1771 was said to have red coats with white waistcoats and breeches.

Connecticut Provincials

In 1709, Connecticut raised a regiment of 365 men sent to the Lake George area. In the following two years 300 men were raised, divided into nine companies in 1710 for the capture of Port Royal, and six – including one of grenadiers – in 1711. That year, clothing from Britain was also supplied to these embodied militiamen, probably in the royal livery colors of red lined with blue.

Connecticut agreed to contribute a regiment of 500 men under Col.Andrew Burr for the 1745 Louisbourg expedition. These men had no uniforms and, once at Louisbourg, many were said to be barefoot and poorly clothed. By July the fortress had fallen; 160 men remained in garrison there, and were eventually incorporated into Shirley's and Pepperell's regiments. Another 300 militiamen were drafted temporarily and sent to New York following the fall of Saratoga in November 1745. A regiment of ten companies of 100 men each under Col.Elisha Williams was raised in June 1746 for the "Canadian expedition." By the onset of fall the regiment was still in Connecticut, as it was clear that there would be no expedition. The men were sent on furlough on October 31, 1746 and given half pay until disbanded a year later. Three companies were raised in 1747 to bolster the garrison of Albany during the winter of 1747–48.

Connecticut's contribution during the Seven Years' War was quite significant; the province raised four numbered regiments almost every year from 1755 to 1760. In 1755, the 1st (Col., later Maj.Gen.Phineas Lyman) and 2nd (Col.Elizur Gooderich) were raised at six, then nine companies each, on service from April to December. The 3rd (Col.Eliphalet Dyer) and 4th (Col.Elihu Chaucey) Regts each had nine companies on service from September to December. In 1756 all four regiments had eight companies from March to December, being

commanded by Lyman, Col.David Wooster, Col.Nathan Whiting an
Col.Andrew Ward respectively. In 1757, however, only a single regimer
of 14 companies was raised from February to December, led by Lyman
In 1758 there were again four regiments, now of 12 companies each, o
service from March to November, commanded by Lyman, Whitin,
Eleazar Fitch and Wooster respectively. In 1759 all four regiments wer
on service from March to December, the 1st and 2nd (Lyman an
Whiting) having first ten and then 13 companies, and the 3rd and 4t
(Wooster and Fitch) having ten, then 12 companies. In 1760 the fou
regiments had 12 companies each, serving from March to Novembe
the commanders did not change after 1759. In 1761 only the first tw
regiments were raised, of 12 companies each, serving from April t
December. In 1762 both regiments had 12 companies, the 1st servin
from March to January 1763 and the 2nd from March to December.

Connecticut provincials served in several campaigns. The 2n
Regiment was at the battle of Lake George in 1755 and served in th
area during the years which followed. The four regiments took part i
the failed campaign against Ticonderoga in July 1758 (see Plate G). The
were at Oswego in 1759–60 and at Crown Point in 1761. In 1762 the 1
Regiment was sent to Havana, where it lost about half its men to yello
fever; the 2nd was at Crown Point. In March 1764 the colony raised
battalion of five companies totaling 265 officers and men, of which 15
under Col.Israel Putnam formed part of Col.Bradstreet's army whic
reached Detroit in August.

RHODE ISLAND

Militia and independent volunteer units

Once settled at Providence from 1636, the colonists gave thought t
defense. In March 1638 the assembly ordered that "every inhabitant c
the Island shall always be provided with one muskett" with it
ammunition and match, as well as a "Sword and rest and Bandeliers, a
completely furnished." At the beginning of the Seven Years' War in th
1750s the militia had about 2,600 men in four regiments totaling som
53 companies "of Trained Bands," who were obliged to muster and trai
twice a year. Each militiaman was to show up with a musket, a sword an
a pound of powder and ball, or be fined two pounds.

There were also a number of volunteer units of cavalry and artiller
The earliest cavalry in Rhode Island appears to have been the Islan
Troop of Horse formed in 1667 at Newport, which disbanded some year
later. The Providence Troop of Horse was raised in 1719, the King
County Troop of Horse in 1730, and a new Newport Troop of Horse i
1746, joined by a 2nd Newport Troop by 1760.

The Artillery Company of Newport was founded on February 1, 174
(see Plate D). An artillery company was raised in Providence in 1744; thi
was redesignated the Providence Cadet Company in August 1774 upo
becoming an infantry unit, "of seventy-five youths, the flower o
Providence. The uniform of this company was scarlet coats, faced wit
yellow" – according to one of its members, Elkanah Watson. Anothe
artillery company was raised in 1755 from men at Westerly an
Charlestown.

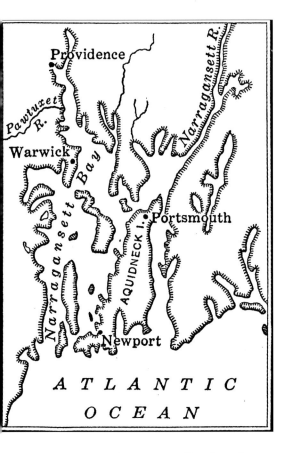

Map of colonial Rhode Island.

An independent infantry company was raised in Newport in 1755; but it was 1774 which saw many more such independent companies suddenly formed at a time of growing political discontent. From August that year there appeared the Providence Light Infantry, the Providence Grenadier Company, the Providence Fusiliers, the North Providence Rangers, a new Providence Artillery Company, the Gloucester Light Infantry and the Pawtuxet Rangers. There was also the Newport Light Infantry, whose "uniform was to be of American manufacture" (*Newport Mercury*, January 23, 1775) with blue facings; and the Kentish Guards in East Greenwich, dressed in red faced with green. Many of these units – along with others just raised, such as the "Warwick Greens" – joined the army under Gen.Washington blockading Boston in late April 1775.

Rhode Island Provincials

Three provincial companies were raised for the Louisbourg expedition in 1745. The following year three companies were again raised, and sent to Annapolis Royal (NS) in October. William Rice, one of the provincial soldiers, recalled receiving 35 dollars "with clothing, arms, ammunition as bounty"; and he later mentioned his "silver-hilted sword" and a "Scarlet velvet cap trimmed with gold," although this could equally have been from the dress of his previous unit, the Newport Troop of Horse.

From March 1755 a 400-man regiment was raised, reinforced by three companies of 50 men each in May and again by 200 men in September,

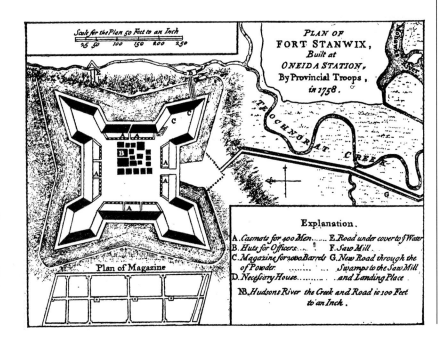

Plan of Fort Stanwix, built on the shores of the Mohawk River by provincial troops in 1758. It was built to stop French incursions from that route, and as a staging point for the invasion of Canada. Colonel John Whiting's Rhode Island Provincial Regiment served there in 1761.

giving a total of 11 companies. Some were deployed at Forts Edward and William Henry until disbanded in December, except for 185 kept in service (72 in the NY forts). In February 1756 a ten-company regiment of 500 men was raised, reinforced by 100 men in May, reorganized into a 400-man regiment under Col.Benjamin Wickham, and disbanded in November. In February 1757 a 450-man regiment under Col.Samuel Angel was raised; from its ranks a 70-strong company of Rangers was authorized raised on September 19. Rhode Island authorized 250 men to serve at Fort Edward during the winter. In March 1758, Col.Henry Babcock's regiment of 1,000 men was raised and was part of Gen.Abercromby's army defeated at Ticonderoga on July 8; 318 men took part in Bradstreet's capture of Fort Frontenac in August. Babcock's was reraised from February 26, 1759, serving with Gen.Amherst's army; and again in 1760, under Col.Christopher Harris, when it served at Crown Point. The establishment went from 1,000 to 666 between April and November 1761, serving under Col.John Whiting at Fort Stanwix; 64 men were retained for duty until July 1763. The 666-man regiment was again raised in 1762 under Col.Samuel Rose, 436 men being posted to Fort Stanwix and 217 to Havana.

From February 1755 a company to garrison Fort George at Newport was also raised by the province, and served there until June 1763.

Rhode Island provincials appear to have had no uniforms. An idea of some of these soldiers' appearance may be gained from the description of a 1760 deserter of the Rhode Island Provincial Regiment; supposedly out recruiting, he instead ran off with "a considerable sum of money," while wearing a "brown colored coat, a green corded everlasting jacket, blue plush breeches, a dark brown cut wig, sometimes wears a cockade in his hat, large open work silver buckles in his shoes, and a silver watch in his pocket" (*New York Mercury*, May 5, 1760).

MARYLAND

Militia
This colony was founded in 1634 by refugee English Catholics under a charter obtained by Lord Baltimore from King Charles I. Each Maryland "adventurer" was to have a musket, a bandolier with a powder flask, a sword, a belt and ammunition. By 1638 the St. Mary's settlement had its

(continued on page 33

Fort Frederick, Maryland. The fort was built near the Potomac River from May 1756 by order of the legislature of Maryland to protect its western settlers from the French and Indians. Unlike most frontier forts, which could be burned, Fort Frederick was built of stone with walls three feet thick and 20 feet high. It was never attacked, and served as an important staging point for Forbes' 1758 campaign against Fort Duquesne. Some 700 terrorstruck settlers crowded into the fort in 1763 during Pontiac's uprising. (Photo: RC)

1: Connecticut militiaman, c.1637
2: Sergeant, Governor's Guard, Massachusetts, 1630s–40s
3: Militiaman, Boston Train of Artillery, c.1638

A

1: Musketeer, New England
   Companies, 1675–76
2: Trooper, Massachusetts Militia
   Horse, 1670s–90s
3: Officer, Massachusetts Militia,
   c.1675

B

1: Trooper, Albany Troop of Horse,
   New York, 1687
2: Trooper, Somerset County Dragoons,
   Maryland, 1690s
3: Musketeer, Dorchester Company,
   Massachusetts, 1690

C

1: Officer, New England Provincials, Louisbourg, 1745
2: Officer, Maryland Militia, c.1745–55
3: Gunner, Newport Artillery Company, Rhode Island, 1740s

D

1: Private, New York Provincial Regiment, 1757
2: Grenadier, Albany Militia Regiment, c.1745–63
3: Officer, Boston Militia Regiment, c.1750–60

1

2

3

1: Private, New Jersey Provincial Regiment,
   1755–58
2: Private, Maryland Provincial Companies, 1757
3: Officer, Massachusetts Provincial Regiments,
   1757–60

1

2

3

F

1: Officer, New York Provincial Regiment, 1758
2: Officer, 2nd Connecticut Provincial Regiment, c.1758
3: Private, Massachusetts Provincial
   Regiments, 1757–60

G

1: Private, Boston Independent Company of Cadets, 1772
2: Gunner, Independent Artillery Co of New London, Connecticut, 1762
3: Officer, 11th New Hampshire Militia Regiment, 1774

1

2

3

...ined band of 120 men; ...d in the early 1640s ...otains were appointed for ...very hundred" men. In ...oril 1650 the Maryland ...gislative assembly allowed ...full-time garrison of six ...en under a captain in the ...rt at St. Inigo harbor. ...ere were few threats ... the early settlers of ...aryland, the local Indians ...ving sold the land to ...em and moved away.

...In March 1655 the ...lony was shaken by civil ...ife between Puritans and ...tholics, and the Catholics ...re defeated with some 40 men killed at a battle on the Severn River.

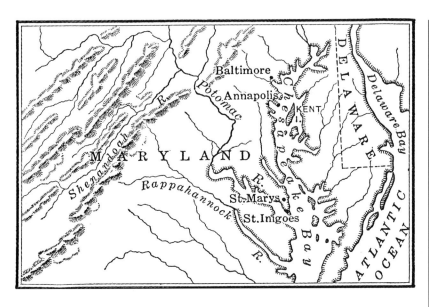

Map of colonial Maryland.

...e militia was later ordered to disarm any inhabitant suspected of ...saffection towards the colony's government – which meant Catholics, ...uakers and Baptists, who were henceforth denied the rights of ...izenship until the Revolution.

On July 12, 1658 the militia companies were gathered into two ...giments, the Northern and the Southern. Able-bodied men from 16 to ... years of age were to have arms and hold monthly musters; fines on ...faulters would pay for the purchase of drums and colors. There was ...o a "governor's own company" which was not part of either regiment. ...e first detailed militia law was passed by the provincial legislature in ...61. Five years later the province purchased 140 snaphance muskets, ...0 cutlasses and belts, 50 carbines "for Horsemen" and ammunition, as ...reserve of weapons for its militia.

As the colony grew, county regiments were organized and, by ...e 1690s, these often had troops of cavalry and dragoons ...ongside their infantry companies. At least one troop of dragoons

Fort Frederick's stone walls were not embanked with earth inside but had wooden galleries running along the top, as shown in this reconstruction. The fort was restored from the 1920s. (Photo: RC)

...s fully equipped with ...ms and accoutrements ...ported from England ...e Plate C). From 1692 ...few "Maryland Rangers" ...re posted in three ...ontier forts. The colony ...ntinued to buy arms ...d ammunition for ...any years through a ...x on tobacco exports, ...hough the practice ...came a major cause of ...ntention between the ...gislative assembly and ...e governor in the late ...30s.

With warfare raging in the Ohio country on its western borders from 1754, Maryland was faced for the first time with a major threat. Some volunteer units were raised, notably at Fort Garrison, where Capt.John Risteau mobilized men of the Baltimore County Militia in July 1755; meanwhile the "Bladensburg Independents" were issued with "55 new firelocks, slings, cartouch boxes and bayonets." In September "the inhabitants of Baltimore" purchased "by subscription, a quantity of Carbines, Bayonets, and Cartouch Boxes" which were preserved in a "Publick Repository, for the Defense of that flourishing place" (*Boston Evening Post*, September 1, 1755). Some men were clearly preparing for duty, as "20 firelocks" were issued to the "Baltimore Volunteers" in October.

On August 30, 1756 the governor ordered a company of militiamen from each county of Prince George and Baltimore to Fort Frederick for one month's service: they departed in late October, "well equipped" and "at their own expense." Much later, in December 1774, a company of Independent Cadets was raised in Baltimore and uniformed in a (possibly red?) coat with buff facings and yellow buttons, white stockings and black half-boots.

Maryland Provincials

Three companies of provincial soldiers were raised for the expedition against Canada in 1747. They were provided with 300 muskets having slings and bayonets, 300 "cartouch boxes with belts," six drums, six halberds for sergeants and nine half-pikes for the officers.

The trouble on the western frontiers in 1754 moved Governor Horatio Sharpe to authorize the raising of an infantry company under Capt.John Dagsworthy on August 7 that year. By September it had 50 or 60 men, and was sent to stand guard at Fort Cumberland for the winter. They were armed with muskets, "slings, cartouch boxes and bayonets." In July 1755 the company was with Gen.Braddock's army. Following Braddock's defeat, the Maryland legislature authorized 80 men to serve on the frontier for four months.

In May 1756 two companies of 100 men each were authorized to garrison the western frontier; the men raised were armed, provisioned and – a new feature – clothed by the province, and were to serve until February 1757. In October 1756 another company of 100 men was added to serve until the next April. In February 1757 the two initial companies were ordered kept in service at Fort Frederick until April. In May 1757 the number of troops in provincial service was raised to 500, divided into five companies (see Plate F). This must have

This small squared log cabin in Fort Cumberland (Cumberland, MD) was used by the Virginia provincial commander Maj.George Washington as his headquarters during 1754. It was surrounded by a stockade in September of that year, and other structures were added later. Maryland provincials were in garrison from the fall of 1754. The fort was abandoned following the fall of Fort Duquesne in late 1758. (Photo: RC)

been judged too expensive since, after heated debate, the legislature finally agreed to a compromise and approved a force of 300 men to serve during 1758. Some served with Forbes' army marching against Fort Duquesne, and about 100 were with Maj.Grant's force which was routed by the French and Indians near that fort in September. They helped defend Fort Ligonier when the French and Indians under Capt.Aubry raided it on October 15.

Ultimately, the outnumbered French abandoned and blew up Fort Duquesne. The 300-man provincial force was renewed until April 1759, stationed at Fort Frederick and ordered to "act as rangers for the Security and Protection of the Frontier Inhabitants." Thereafter, the colony did not raise provincial troops; but two companies of Maryland volunteers in Pennsylvania's pay were with Col.Bouquet's expedition against Pontiac's Indians in October 1764.

NEW YORK

Militia

Following the surrender of the Dutch in 1664, the British authorities issued orders for organizing the militia into companies. "All males above sixteen" were to be enrolled, each armed with a musket, a sword, a bandolier, a priming horn and another horn for coarse powder. In July 1667 the governor of New York, Col.Nicolls, ordered that one-third of the militia companies "now afoot" in the countryside should provide themselves with horses, saddles and arms so as to be "ready at an hour's warning," since a French incursion was feared. By November a third of the militia had reportedly been converted into companies of horse and dragoons (CSPC 1667).

After the short period of renewed Dutch rule in 1673–74, New York became definitively British, and its 1677 Militia Act repeated the requirement to have one-third of its 2,000 militiamen mounted. This was unrealistic, and as time passed such numbers could not be met; most of the early settlers could not afford the horses, tack .and equipment. According to Jaspar Dankers and Peter Sluyter, who traveled to New York City in 1679, the "training and muster" they saw on May 8 "had not taken place before in two years, because the small-pox had prevailed so much last year. Some were on horseback, and six small companies were on foot. They were exercised in military tactics, but I have never seen anything worse of the kind. They comprised all the forces of New York [city] and the adjacent places."

Ten years later the New York militia had to deal with the political tensions resulting from the Glorious Revolution in England during 1688, with the consequent flight of King James II and the accession to the throne of his daughter Mary in

Nicholas William Stuyvesant (1648–98), son of the famous Dutch governor Peter, shown mounted in an amusingly naive 1666 painting made in New York. This work gives an idea of the many mounted militias in New York at the time. Stuveysant is shown in a dark coat (possibly black), white cravat, cuffs and fold-over stockings, black shoes with red heels and soles, black hat, and with a red saddle cloth edged gold. (Print after Henri Couturier)

co-sovereignty with her Dutch husband, William III of Orange. It was from 1689, however, with the declaration of war between France and Britain ("King William's War"), that the New Yorkers were called to arms. Their Mohawk allies often raided the French in Canada, culminating in the destruction of the village of Lachine near Montreal in August 1689 and the slaughter of many of its settlers. The horror-stricken Canadians vowed revenge and, in February 1690, Schenectady was devastated with equal cruelty by the Canadians and their Indian allies, who also razed several other New England towns.

The countryside north of Albany was the most threatened, and part of the militia was mobilized to stand watch against the small parties of Indian raiders which now infested the area. Some reinforcements were sent from New York City to Albany, as well as some stores. Ammunition, with 47 "fire lockes & Bandalier with 1 halbert, 1 Pike heading, 1 Drum" and a "Jack" flag had been sent in November 1689. In March 1690 more supplies apparently for 200 men, were sent from New York City; these included "2100 ells of Brown osenburg" cloth, "100 drest dear skins" and "180 Kartrit [cartridge] Boxes," while the city of Albany came up with another 100 dressed deerskins, "60 gunns" and "100 Hatchets" (DHNY, II).

How these supplies were used is difficult to say. Many militiamen showed up with their own arms and probably all with their own clothes. The dressed deerskins could be used in a variety of ways; some of the brown "osenburg" cloth could have been used for making new clothing, and the halberds and drums were for standard garrison duties. The Albany volunteer militiamen who ventured with Capt.John Schuyler to raid the outskirts of Montreal in August 1690, and with Capt.Peter Schuyler in 1691, would have had a mixture of European and Indian clothing and equipment suitable for such "woods-running." The Schuylers' daring initiatives remained isolated episodes.

The 1691 militia law for New York colony decreed that every foot soldier was to have: "a well fixed Musquet or Fusee, or if the Officer so appoint, with a good Pike, or Sword, or Lance and Pistol; each Musqueteer six Charges of Powder, and one Cartouch Box" along with gun tools and ammunition.

New York militiamen, like those of other colonies, retained a basically European-style garrison role. This was followed carefully in Albany which was the largest town to the north; it had a bastioned fort and was enclosed by a palisade ten feet high. In the early 1690s its independent company of regular "redcoats" was bolstered by 30 to 40 mobilized and paid militiamen. Another 300 city militiamen could be called up, and about 700 men from the immediate area. When, in February 1693, the French and Canadian Indians attacked the

A model of Albany in the 1690s. It was protected by a ten-foot-high palisade. On the height which dominated the town stood Fort Frederick, which was also the governor's residence. (Albany Visitor Center)

Mohawk "castles" north of Albany, the alarm was such that 150 New York City militiamen, 120 from Queen's County and 50 from King's County volunteered and went to Albany, some going further to reinforce Schenectady. Major Schuyler led 250 men (including 50 mounted troopers) from Albany and 290 Mohawks in an attempt to catch the raiders. There was a skirmish with the enemy as they retreated after devastating the Mohawk castles, but the pursuit was given up on account of shoes being quite wore out and provisions scarce."

In 1696 Count Frontenac mounted a major French expedition that devastated Onondaga villages and crops. No English soldiers or militiamen were there to help them repulse the attack; indeed, there was even some difficulty for the Iroquois in obtaining arms and ammunition from Albany. In view of these disasters the Iroquois chiefs concluded that the British colonists could not protect them; with their people now perishing from famine, they entered negotiations with the French. This led to the "Great Peace of 1701" concluded in Montreal, a masterstroke by the French which ensured for New France reasonably peaceful relations with the Indians for half a century.

New York colony was especially affected by the neutralization of the Iroquois. The hinterland stretching south from Lake Champlain to south of Lake George and west along the southern shore of Lake Ontario was now something of a neutral area. New York's influence north of Schenectady was minimal, and it would increasingly have to count on its own forces for its defence. In November 1700 the militia mustered some 3,182 men, divided into the county regiments of Suffolk, Queen's, King's, Richmond, West Chester, the combined Ulster and Duchess County, the city and county of New York, and the city and county of Albany. There were troops of horse in the towns of New York and Albany and in the counties of Queen's, King's, Ulster and Duchess. Despite these numbers, the colony was ill-prepared for trouble; no arms and ammunition were held in reserve, and no militia training took place in the early 18th century.

War with France broke out again in 1702, and New York mobilized 150 men as fusiliers and 30 scouts to guard the northern frontier against raids in the summer of 1703. More were occasionally posted on such duty in the years to come and, in 1709, the colony also raised three provincial regiments (see below).

In the following decades New York would depend mainly on the few British regulars posted at Albany and, from the 1720s, at Fort Oswego – the colony's major and largely successful attempt to retain British influence on the southern shore of Lake Ontario. The province's militia nevertheless grew to 8,798 men including 423 officers by 1737. In 1774 New York had about 32,000 militiamen in 26 infantry regiments, 11 troops of cavalry and a few artillery companies.

Captain Johannes – or John – Schuyler (1668–1747) of Albany, New York, portrayed in c.1715. He was the son of Maj.Peter Schuyler, a leading figure in the early militia of Albany. Captain Schuyler led the daring 1690 raid on Laprairie near Montreal, and became mayor of Albany in 1703. He is shown in an all-brown velvet suit with brown buttons, with a plain black hat under his arm, a powdered wig, and a gilt-hilted sword indicating his officer's status in the militia. (Print after an anonymous painting probably made in New York City)

As in other colonies, the New York militia units were required to have colors or standards and drums or trumpets. The great majority did not have uniforms, although all were supposed to have weapons according to militia laws. However, in major towns and settlements there were a few well-equipped units which attracted the keener volunteers.

A few cavalry troops in the major towns had uniforms. In 1685 the Albany Troop of Horse, formed in March of that year, was mentioned wearing blue duffel coats (see Plate C). The uniform required in 1721 for each New York City trooper was a scarlet coat trimmed with silver lace, a silver-laced hat, black hair bags or ribbons, a pair of boots with spurs, and a carbine; he was to turn out fully armed and equipped on horse at least 14 hands high. In 1744 the city's troopers changed to blue coats with gold buttons and gold lace, scarlet waistcoats, blue breeches and gold-laced hats. The uniform remained unchanged until the eve of the American Revolution: in 1772 the New York Militia Law prescribed for the "New York Troop of Horse, City and County of New York" a uniform consisting of a "Blue Coat and Breeches, with yellow Metal Buttons, and a scarlet Waistcoat, and their Hats laced with Gold Lace." Meanwhile, the Albany Troop of Horse continued to wear blue; in 1736 it had blue coats with silver-laced hats, and this was still the lawfully prescribed dress in 1772. The King's County Troop of Horse had blue coats, red jackets (waistcoats) and silver-laced hats at that time.

New York City had a "Blue Artillery Company" from 1709, its name inspired by the color of its coats. It had four small field pieces with some Coehorn mortars; by 1738 it boasted five officers including Capt.John Waldron, and 81 artillerymen. Following the news of the fall of Fort William Henry to Montcalm in 1757, the company formed part of a 700-man force sent as reinforcements to Albany in August. The "Blue" company remained in existence during the American War of Independence. In 1775 it was redesignated "1st Company of Royal

Artillery, City and County of New York" under Capt.Samuel Tudor, and had a blue uniform with "Red facings White under Cloaths &c."

A few elite city infantry units made up of well-to-do volunteers did provide themselves with uniforms from about the middle of the 18th century. The New York City Grenadiers wore blue and red coats with grenadier caps. The grenadier company of the Albany militia infantry also wore the same colors (see Plate E).

New York Provincials

For the projected invasion of Canada in 1709, three provincial regiments were organized under Cols.Schuyler, Whiting and Mathews. They probably wore the clothing in the royal colors (red faced with blue) sent from England, and there was also an order for 250 red caps for their grenadiers to be made in the colony. The regiments were disbanded following the cancellation of the expedition.

New York raised 29 companies of 100 men each which served from June 1746 to November 24, 1747; two Indian companies totaling 41 officers and men were also in service from August 1746 to November 24, 1747. They were armed, equipped but apparently not uniformed.

The New York Provincial Regiment was first raised in May 1755 as a single battalion of 800 officers and men; it was re-raised in 1756 to 1,715 officers and men, and again in 1757 (see Plate E). In August that year part of it was badly mauled during and after the siege and fall of Fort William Henry by Montcalm. A peak was reached in March 1758 when the New York assembly voted for a three-battalion regiment totaling 2,680 officers and men under a colonel-commandant. Oliver De Lancey, brother of New York governor James De Lancey, was commissioned to lead the regiment. The unit served with Gen.Abercromby's army during the failed attempt on Ticonderoga in July 1758, but it participated in the capture of Fort Frontenac in late August (see Plate G).

In 1759 and 1760 the regiment was raised to the same strength but divided into two battalions. It took part in the siege and capture of Fort Niagara in July 1759, and was part of Gen.Amherst's army at the surrender of Montreal in September 1760. In 1761 it was reduced to 1,787 officers and men who were posted as garrisons at Oswego, and had more than 900 men at Oswego and 567 at Havana in 1762.

In early 1763 some 173 officers and men were raised to garrison frontier forts, some being killed on September 14 by Pontiac's Indians near Fort Niagara. On December 13, 1763 the New York assembly voted to raise 300 men to "be employed against the enemy Indians," 173 to garrison frontier forts and 300 to guard the western frontier. They were "to be clothed in a light manner: a cloth jacket, flannel waistcoat, leggins, etc. will be sufficient; & it will be necessary that the whole be raised, and

William Johnson (1715–74) as colonel of the 2nd Battalion the Albany County Militia when he was appointed Superintendent of Indian Affairs 1754, and major-general commanding the forces for the expedition against Crown Point 1755. He was wounded at the battle of Lake George on September 8, but the victory earned him a knighthood. In 1759 he led the forces that took Fort Niagara. A talented diplomat and genuine admirer of the Native Americans, he was invaluable in rallying the Indians to the British side. He is shown in this miniature in an all-scarlet coat and white waistcoat with gold buttons and lace. In June 1754 he ordered two coats with green velvet lapels and cuffs, green light material for lining the coats and two waistcoats, white buttons for the coats, gilt buttons for the waistcoats, and enough silver lace for one coat and waistcoat (PWJ, I). The color of the coats and waistcoats is not given. (National Archives of Canada, C83497)

Map of colonial New Jersey, divided into East and West Jersey, and of adjoining colonies.

ready to proceed to Albany the 1st of March next... [A]nd they shall likewise be provided with arms, unless any of them choose to bring their own arms." Some 180 were part of Bradstreet's expedition to Detroit in the summer of 1764.

NEW JERSEY

Militia

Initially part of New Netherlands, the settlements in New Jersey became predominantly English as more colonists settled there from 1664. They were under no threat, and New Jersey's main military role in the colonial wars was to support the colony of New York. The Militia Act passed on July 8, 1730 called for every man from 16 to 60 years of age to be enrolled and to be armed with "one good sufficient Musquet, or Fuzee, well fixt," a sword or bayonet, a cartouch box or powder horn, a half-pound of powder and 12 balls. There were no specifications regarding how the militia was to be organized.

War with Spain in 1739–40 spurred the legislative assembly to vote $1,309 for "[feeding] and transporting the Troops to be raised in this Colony" for an expedition to the West Indies. About 300 men were raised, obviously recruits for Gooch's Regiment. In 1755--56 about 13,000 men were "mustered and trained every six months and to appear, every man with a good firelock etc. fit to march against the enemy" (PRO/WO 34/101).

New Jersey Provincials

In June 1746 the assembly passed an act to encourage the enlistment of 500 "Freemen or Native well affected Indians" for an expedition against Canada, and some $7,000 was voted to arm and clothe these men. By September the men had been organized into five companies of 100 men each. These provincial soldiers were reported to be "full of vigor and Spirit, being completely [clothed and fed], and well provided with muskets [and] Cutlasses," according to the *Pennsylvania Gazette*. Peter Schuyler was named colonel. Once in Albany the New Jersey troops were beset by problems, however. In November came complaints that 300 of the muskets furnished were rusted and pitted, that many swords were of bad quality, that the breeches were shoddy and that the commissioners who purchased the arms and clothing had lined their own pockets. In February 1747 the commissioners replied, claiming that the "Coats were of blue Cloth and breeches of red Halfthicks" and were "the most durable Wear we have from Europe." There was also a further supply of "a Pair of Buckskin Breeches" to each man (*New York Gazette*, April 6, 1747). At that time, Col.Schuyler wrote that the "regiment" was in good health but lacked shirts, flints and colors. It also lacked money: in May

1747 the five companies "mutinied" because they had not been paid. Nevertheless, in the face of the threat from the French and Indians the New Jersey troops marched to Saratoga, serving until October 31, 1747.

From April 22, 1755, New Jersey raised a provincial regiment of five companies of 100 men each, again under the command of Col.Peter Schuyler. In 1756 half of the regiment was in Schenectady and the other half at Oswego with Col.Schuyler. In early July, Oswego was besieged by Montcalm's French army; the fort surrendered on the 14th and its garrison was taken to Canada. Command passed to Capt.Peter Parker, but the regiment's bad luck persisted. On July 21, 1757 it was badly mauled by the French and Indians at Sabbath Day Point, and in August the 301 remaining officers and men of the regiment were all captured by Montcalm at Fort William Henry, being paroled for 18 months.

The colony of New Jersey did not give up, however, and re-raised the regiment under the command of Col.John Johnson from March 25, 1758, with 1,000 men divided into ten companies including one of grenadiers. It marched north and, in June, were said to be "the likeliest well-set of men for the Purpose as has been perhaps turned out on any Campaign" by the *New York Mercury* (see Plate F). Over 400 of its men took part in Abercromby's bungled assault on Ticonderoga on July 8, 1758, and participated in the capture of Fort Frontenac in late August. The following year, once again under the command of Col.Schuyler, the New Jersey Regiment was deployed further west and finally took part in a victorious campaign, that against Fort Niagara in July. In 1760 it was mostly posted at Oswego, but joined Gen.Amherst's army in August and was thus present at the surrender of Montreal the following month. Capt.Knox noted the "Jersey Blues" as "a well disciplined, regular corps" made up of "a good body of men" making "a respectable appearance."

The regiment had 600 men from 1761, and was mostly posted at Oswego and Niagara until 1762, when some 222 men were sent to Havana. A detachment escorting supplies near Oswego was lost to Pontiac's Indians on September 14, 1763. In November that year the 600-strong regiment was renewed until the uprising ended. About 151 men served with Bradstreet's expedition to Detroit in the summer of 1764. On the whole, and in spite of its unfortunate early campaigns, this regiment was considered one of the best equipped and best disciplined units in the American colonies.

A volunteer company of 66 officers and men was also embodied from November 1, 1761 for a year's service, probably at Oswego. They were to have a blanket, a blue watchcoat, cloth, check and white shirts, a pair of cloth and a pair of ticken breeches, pairs of yarn stockings, shoes, a felt hat, arms and accoutrements.

Colonel Peter Schuyler of the New Jersey Regiment, c.1755–56. Blue coat and breeches, scarlet cuffs, lapels, lining and waistcoat, gold buttons and gold lace edging the waistcoat. Sketch by C.C.P.Lawson after an anonymous portrait. (Anne S.K. Brown Military Collection, Brown University. Photo: RC)

THE PLATES

A1: Connecticut militiaman, c.1637

The various settlements were ordered to provide 50 corselets for the 90 militiamen raised by Capt.John Mason in early May 1637, although the men otherwise provided their own arms and equipment. When they stormed the Pequot stronghold on May 23, Capt.John Underhill mentioned that they were all "completely armed with corselets," which would indicate that the remaining 40 or so men had gotten all the armor they could lay hands on. Their armor would have included at least breast- and back-plates; it seems many also had helmets – these would be any morrion, cabasset, or pikeman's "pot" available. Underhill described the ferocious fight that ensued in which his companion Capt.Mason "received many arrows against his [headpiece]," while he himself was shot by an arrow "through a sufficient Buffe coate" and another arrow "received between the neck and shoulders, hanging between the lining of my [headpiece]." Others were hit in the face, on the head, through the shoulders and in the legs. (John Underhill, *Newes From America AD 1638*)

A2: Sergeant, Governor's Guard, Massachusetts Militia, 1630s–40s

In colonial Massachusetts ceremonial functions had an important role from the outset. In 1635 the General Court provided itself with a "Governor's Guard" consisting of six sergeants armed with halberds and swords, who served during the ceremonial first day of the legislature's session, their numbers being reduced to two thereafter. The pikemen, with their impressive armor, were the obvious choice to provide such guards whenever possible. The guardsmen were embodied on active duty for the time required and their number varied as occasion warranted. In 1643, when Governor La Tour of French Acadia showed up in Boston for a courtesy visit escorted by 40 soldiers, the surprised Massachusetts authorities mobilized the militia and multiplied the guard to impress the visitors.

A3: Militiaman, Boston Train of Artillery, c.1638

The early dress of this unit was mentioned as "buff," which agrees with the early dress of the London Artillery Garden – later the Honourable Artillery Company – after which the Boston unit was patterned. As many of the Boston unit's early members had been in the London company, it can safely be assumed that its dress would have been much the same: a buff leather coat over a red cloth coat, red breeches and a red helmet plume. The unit's founder, Capt.Robert Keane, stressed the importance of training and, as late as 1653, favored the purchase of "Pikes & Bandal[ie]rs." He left money in his will for "the erecting of a platform[e] planked

Pikeman's armor. c.1620–50. Such armor was especially used in Massachusetts. (Harold L. Peterson Coll., Jamestown National Historic Park, Virginia)

underneath for two mounted peeces of Ordnance to stand upon... in the most convenient p[oin]t in the Trayning place in Boston." He also recalled that the company always had a better and "more constant appearance then when fynes were duly taken for late & non-appearance." By the late 17th or early 18th century the dress changed: in 1738 "our scarlet and crimson" was mentioned, which, according to an 1820 history of the unit, meant that "the dress of the company was very rich, such as a scarlet coat, crimson silk stockings with large gold clocks [sic], and shoes with silver buckles; also a large cocked hat trimmed with gold lace." The stockings were white from September 2, 1754. The major change came on September 9, 1756 when the members of the company voted that they would provide themselves to henceforth appear in "a blue coat and a gold-laced hat." Gaiters only came into wear from April 2, 1770, when white "spatterdashes" with white buttons and black knee bands were approved. On July 28, 1772 the uniform was ordered to be "blue coats and lapels, with yellow buttons, the cock of the hat to be uniform with the militia officers; – wigs and hair to be clubbed." The company had a band of music at that time, uniformed in "a white cloth coat, with blue lapels, trimmed with blue and white linings; white linen waistcoat and breeches, and a cap covered with white cloth and trimmed with gold binding." Until about 1768–70 the officers had half-pikes but then replaced them with espontoons. Sergeants had halberds but did not wear swords until 1790. (Z.G.Whitman, *An Historical Sketch of the Ancient and Honourable Artillery Company*, Boston, 1820; J.H.Leslie, "The will of Captain Robert Keane," *JSAHR*, VI, 1927)

B1: Musketeer, New England Companies, 1675–76

During King Philip's War many militiamen from Massachusetts, Plymouth Bay, Connecticut and Rhode Island were sent on active service against the Indians. The infantry successfully adapted to fighting in woods and swamps; the men were dressed in their everyday clothes, though for protection many had buff coats. Arms consisted of flintlock (or "doglock") muskets, swords and hatchets; bandoliers were not carried because of the rattling noise made by the wooden "cartridges." (Frank E.Southard, Jr., "Military Organization in Maine's First Indian War," *MC&H*, XI, Summer 1960; George A.Snook & Eric Manders, "New England Independent Companies, 1675–1676," *MC&H*, XVI, Summer 1964)

B2: Trooper, Massachusetts Militia Horse, 1670s–90s

During the 1670s and 1680s the troops of horses in Massachusetts Bay were said to have been "all well mounted and completely armed with back, breast, headpiece, buff coats, sword, carbine and pistols. Each of the twelve troops then in the colony was distinguished by their coats." The last phrase may mean either that the buff leather coats distinguished them, since another account mentioned that they wear buff coats, pistols, hangers, and corselets;" or that each trooper also made an effort to wear a cloth coat of an agreed color for the troop; or both. The standard helmet was the triple-barred lobster-tail type, used since the 1640s and painted black (as was the body armor) to protect them from rust. In any event, armor and buff coats were consistent with the English cavalry of the day. During King Philip's War, Capt.Prentice's troop of horse from Newton gave signal service, so that "his name was a terror to the hostile tribes of Indians; by suddenly collecting and marching his cavalry at the shortest notice, fighting on horseback or on foot..." Buff coats were still very protective. At an engagement in June 1675, Trooper Gill of Capt.Prentice's troop "was struck by a musket ball on the side of his body, but being clad with a buff coat, and some thickness of paper under it, it never broke his skin." (CSPC 1675; "History of Newton," *Collections of the Massachusetts Historical Society*, 1798; B.Church, *History of King Phillip's War*, Boston, 1865)

B3: Officer, Massachusetts Militia, c.1675

This figure is based on the portrait by Thomas Smith of Capt. George Curwen (1610–85) of Salem and on his probate inventory of February 1685. Curwen was a wealthy merchant and prominent militiaman who commanded the Salem troops of Horse in 1666. His extensive wardrobe included a coat "with silver lace," a "Tropeing scarfe [or sash] and hat band," rapiers "Tipt wth. Silver," a "buff belt wth. Silver buckles," 4 muskets, "1 pr. Pistolls & Holsters, 1 plush Sadle layed wth. Silver lace & Sadle Cloth." In Puritan Massachusetts the "newe and immodest fashions" of gold and silver lace and embroidery were frowned upon. Officers were chosen from among the elite and their dress was not as "sad," since they were not subject to the Massachusetts sumptuary laws provided their estate was worth more than £200. (*Collections of the Massachusetts Historical Society*, 1798; G.F.Dow, *Everyday Life in Massachusetts Bay Colony*, Boston, 1935; painting in the Essex Institute, Salem, MA)

C1: Trooper, Albany Troop of Horse, New York Militia, 1687

One of the earliest mentions of uniform dress for colonial American troops occurred in 1685 when the Albany Troop of Horse, formed in March of that year, was reported wearing blue "duffel coats." Commanded by Capt.George Lockheart, the troop's two officers and 36 troopers were on service from October 5, 1687 to August 1, 1688. They would also have worn hats, waistcoats, breeches, riding boots or gaiters and been armed with a sword and pistols. The unit was transformed "into Dragoons by the Governor" before April 1693. (*DHSNY*, I; Alan & Barbara Aimone, "New York's Provincial Militia," *MC&H*, XXXII, Summer 1981)

C2: Trooper, Somerset County Dragoons, Maryland Militia, 1690s

A troop of Maryland Dragoons was shipped arms and

Major Thomas Savage (1640–1705) of the Boston Militia, 1679. Savage was considered "chief in the soldier's affection, being the only field officer that faced the Indians" during King Philip's War (CSPC 1676). He wears a buff coat with embroidered wide collar and cuffs, a bunch of dark red ribbons on his right shoulder, a crimson waist sash, an embroidered sword baldric, and has embroidery at his shirt cuffs. At left of the portrait, three small figures hold company colors.

equipment purchased from England in 1695. The dragoons were armed with carbines having "round locks and varnished stocks" with "carbine belts and swivels," and "cartouch boxes and belts" as well as "horse pistols, [with] round locks varnished stocks & brass caps," which no doubt went into the holsters of their dragoon saddles. The troop had "6 dragoon drums" and "6 brass trumpets" for its musicians, and carried a small "union flag" as its standard, which may identify it as belonging to Somerset County. No clothing was mentioned and no "uniform" is known. However, members of the troop would have been men of some means, and they were probably asked to parade wearing a red coat – the color worn by English dragoons – which all probably had in their wardrobe, with hats, breeches and boots suitable for riding. (H.C.McBarron & H.L.Peterson, "Maryland Dragoons circa 1695," *MC&H*, III, March 1951)

C3: Musketeer, Dorchester Company, Massachusetts Militia, 1690

Sir William Phips' 1690 expedition to capture Quebec was repulsed by Count Frontenac, and the Massachusetts militiamen traveled home in October; four ships were lost on the way. In 1995 a very old wreck was found in the St. Lawrence River off Anse-aux-Bouleaux east of Quebec City, and identified as one of the lost vessels, possibly the *Elizabeth and Mary* or the *Hannah and Mary*. Several objects recovered belonged to Cornelius Tileston and Increase Mosley, both militiamen in a company from Dorchester, near Boston: the company had vanished without a trace on a small ship for 305 years. The weapons and equipment found in the wreck revealed much variety and featured several older type matchlock muskets. A cartridge box, possibly worn on a waistbelt, was also found. The militiamen of the time wore their own clothing. (*1690: L'attaque de Québec... Une épave raconte*, Montreal, 2000)

D1: Officer, New England Provincials, Louisbourg, 1745

The 4,070 men recruited into the seven Massachusetts, one Connecticut and one New Hampshire regiments, as well as the train of artillery, are not known to have had any specific military uniforms. The men had their own clothing, and brown coats and breeches with a red waistcoat seems to have been a popular choice, at least for officers. It is seen in portraits of Samuel Waldo (see page 12), who was brigadier-general on the expedition as well as colonel of the 2nd Massachusetts Regt; and in that of Lt.John Marston (1715–86) of Moulton's 3rd Massachusetts Regt, upon which this figure is based. Replacement clothes were few and varied. John Kelley, a private in Moulton's Regt, recalled getting only a greatcoat, a green waistcoat without lining, two check shirts, a pair of breeches, two pairs of stockings and a pair of shoes. (Eric I.Manders & Albert W. Haarmann, "Massachusetts at Louisbourg 1745," *MC&H*, XLIII, Summer 1991; Kelley's memorial in Massachusetts Archives, Vol.74, p.24)

D2: Officer, Maryland Militia, c.1745–55

This figure is based on a portrait of Col.Abraham Barnes (1715–78) of St. Mary's County. Barnes was a wealthy shipper in Annapolis, a member of the legislative assembly, a major in the militia in 1746 and promoted colonel in 1756. As in some of the other colonies, militia officers in Maryland opted for an all-scarlet dress which included the coat, waistcoat and breeches. Colonel Barnes had gold buttons, gorget and sword hilt and a crimson sash over the shoulder. (Portrait by John Wollaston, Corcoran Gallery of Art, Washington, DC)

D3: Gunner, Artillery Company of Newport, Rhode Island, 1740s

The Artillery Company of Newport was founded on February 1, 1741 by 18 of the town's prominent citizens, to be a "nursery school for officers" in the military arts. The

The arms of Maj.Thomas Savage: argent, six lioncels, sable. Crest: out of a coronet, or, a bear's paw raised, sable.

company trained, manned the town's batteries and provided officers for militia units. From April 16, 1744 the company was to be clothed in "blue camblet lin'd with scarlet with yellow mottle buttons with white jacket and white stockings," the rest of the dress and equipment to be as ordered by the commanding officer. "Sergeant to carry halbert – rest of company to carry fuzee guns not less than three foot and a half barrel." Apart from the white waistcoat, its uniform was obviously inspired by that of the Royal Artillery. (Allan Archambault & J.P.Lauth, "Artillery Company of Newport, Rhode Island 1741–1757," *MC&H*, XXXI, Summer 1979)

E1: Private, New York Provincial Regiment, 1755

On May 3, 1755 the legislature allowed each man to have "a good lapelled Coat, a Felt Hat, a Shirt, two Pairs of Ozenbrig Trowsers, a Pair of Shoes, and a Pair of Stockings"; there were "New York Regimentals" in 1756, but the colors of these uniforms remain unknown. In March 1757 a deserter went off wearing "a New York Regimental Coat, which is a dark Drab, the sleeves turned up with middle Drab Cloth, Buckskin Waistcoat and Breeches, dark Worsted Stockings, new Shoes and an old Hat" – the description which forms the basis of this figure. (*Pennsylvania Gazette*, May 15, 1755; March 24, 1757)

E2: Grenadier, Albany Militia Regiment, c.1745–63

A unique artifact, the surviving grenadier cap of the Albany Militia Regiment forms the basis for the reconstruction of this figure. The cap is blue with a scarlet front bearing the full royal arms; a beaver on the scarlet "little flap," the edging lace and other decorative embroidery in white. This cap may date as early as the 1740s since, from 1747, most grenadier caps in the regular army were to have the royal cipher ("GR") and the white horse of Hanover on the little flap. However, militia could largely do as they pleased, and the beaver on the little flap was certainly more appropriate to Albany, a town whose wealth largely relied on the fur trade. The uniform would thus be blue faced with scarlet and trimmed with white lace. (Cap in the Albany Institute of History and Art)

E3: Officer, Boston Militia Regiment, c.1750–60

In general there is scant evidence of uniforms being worn by Massachusetts troops until the middle of the 18th century. It seems fairly certain, however, that officers of the Boston Militia Regiment indulged in scarlet coats, possibly as early as the 1680s, since Col.Thomas Richbell had a "Scarlet coate & Breeches W[i]th Silver Buttons" and two "Rapiers W[i]th Silver hilts & a belt." Boston's leading men of the early 18th century were remembered as "wearing citizen dress somewhat similar" to the Ancient and Honourable Artillery Company, which was scarlet laced with gold. As many of the Boston Regiment's officers had been in the artillery, it seems both units wore the same until at least 1756. This figure is based on the c.1750 portrait of Capt.Thomas Savage (1709–60) painted by Richard Badger. He wears a scarlet coat, waistcoat and breeches, gold buttons, gold lace edging the waistcoat and the hat, crimson sash and a gilt-hilted sword. On April 2, 1772 the officers' uniform of the Boston Brigade was ordered by the colonel to be a coat of "scarlet faced of the same, Lin'd with white" with gilt buttons and buttonholes "bound with gold Prussian binding like the Majors," white waistcoat with gilt buttons and gold buttonholes, "Prussian binding on each breast as low as the pocket flaps," white breeches and stockings, "no spatter dashes, sash and gorget, Black Ribbon about the Neck," hat laced with gold and wig with two curls. (*Army & Navy Chronicle*, 1836)

F1: Private, New Jersey Provincial Regiment, 1755–58

The regiment was nicknamed the "Jersey Blues" because of its blue uniform, which was faced with red. In 1755 it was issued "good lapelled Coats," felt hats, check shirts, leather breeches, stockings, shoes and 500 stands of arms. The 1758 legislation specifically called for a "blue coat, after the Highland manner, Lappel'd and cuffed with red, one pair of ticken Breeches, one Blue ditto of the cloath as their Coat, one Check Shirt, one white ditto, two pairs yarn Stockings, two pairs of Shoes, one Hat to each Man, bound with yellow Binding, one Blanket, one Knapsack, one Hatchet, one Canteen, one Camp Kettle to five Men, a pair of white Spaterdashes," as well as 100 grenadier caps. They were seen in New York wearing "blue, faced with red, grey stockings and Buckskin Breeches" in early June 1758. In 1759 and 1760 the hats and grenadier caps were replaced by leather caps, and in 1761 the headgear was "a hat or cap." (*New York Mercury*, June 12, 1758; *Acts of... New Jersey*, Woodbridge, 1761; H.C.McBarron & F.P.Todd, "The New Jersey Regiment (Jersey Blues) 1755–1764," *MC&H*, V, December 1953)

F2: Private, Maryland Provincial Companies, 1757

From 1756, Maryland provincial soldiers were furnished with "1 Coat, 1 Pair Breeches, 1 Pair Stockings, 2 Shirts, 1 Hat and 1 Pair Shoes," but this appears not to have been a specific uniform but merely basic clothing of any sort. In 1757, descriptions of two deserters from Beall's Company reveal uniform clothing consisting of red coats with white metal buttons and sleeves "turn'd up with black," red breeches, white shirts and hats. The following year the many Marylanders serving with Gen.Forbes appear to have been neglected, at least for cold-weather clothing: Forbes complained in October 1758 that they had "no manner of clothing but one blanket each," and "no shoes, stockings or breeches" or anything else against the "Inclemency of the weather," so that "Flannel Jackets" and blankets were added. (W.H.Browne, ed., *Correspondence of Governor Horatio Sharpe 1753–1757*, Baltimore, 1888; J.Hall Pleasants, ed., *Proceedings and Acts... of Maryland*, Baltimore, 1935, Vols.24–26; J.L.Sowers & R.M.Kimmel, "The Maryland Forces 1756–1759," *MC&H*, XXXI, Summer 1979)

F3: Officer, Massachusetts Provincial Regiments, 1757–60

The dress of Massachusetts officers was relatively uncertain at the beginning of the war. Some appear to have had scarlet uniforms, sometimes faced with light buff, while others had blue coats. By 1757 the provincial clothing was confirmed as blue with scarlet lapels and cuffs. Some officers are recorded as receiving coats with scarlet lapels in October 1757. On May 5, 1759, Capt.Knox noted at Fort Cumberland (frontier of Nova Scotia) that the Massachusetts officers were "sober, modest men" who made "a decent appearance, being clothed in blue faced with scarlet, gilt buttons, laced waistcoats and hats." Portraits of Capt.David Mason and an officer (formerly thought to be Joshua Winslow) by Joseph Blackburn show the blue coat faced with scarlet, gold

Colonel Richard Saltonstall (1703–56), Massachusetts Militia, c.1748. Saltonstall graduated from Harvard in 1722, was commissioned colonel of the militia in 1726, and also went on to represent Haverhill at the legislative General Court. He is shown wearing an all-brown coat, and a grey waistcoat with gold lace and buttons. (Print after Robert Feke)

buttons and gold hat lace. Mason's portrait has a scarlet waistcoat edged with gold lace; the other wears a white waistcoat and buttonholes on both the coat and waistcoat are trimmed with narrow gold lace. In the field the uniforms would be altered. On June 16, 1759 at Fort Edward camp, Ruggle's Regiment was reminded that "Except those on duty, it is expected that the commissioned officers do not wear Scotch bonnets but wear something that they may be distinguished as officers." This implied that everyone wore tricorns. (John Knox, *Journal*; *Orderly Book and Journal of Major John Hawks*, New York, 1911)

G1: Officer, New York Provincial Regiment, 1758

Lieutenant Marinus Willet of the 3rd Battalion, who took part in the Ticonderoga and Frontenac expeditions, described his uniform as "a green coat, trimmed with silver twist, white underclothes and black gaiters, also a cocked hat, with a large black cockade of silk ribbon, together with a silver button and loop." The men of the battalion had been issued green uniforms in May 1758. According to a clothing shipment, the sloop *Catharine* carried from New York City to Albany 861 "Coats common green, faced with green" including 63 sergeants' coats, 870 pairs of leather breeches, 1,740 shirts half check and half white, 1,740 pairs of shoes, 863 pairs of green Indian stockings, 864 yarn stockings, 768 hats, 870 canteens, 1,250 haversacks "the overplusage to

Captain John Clarke (1701–64). Clarke was a merchant and militia officer at Salem, Massachusetts. He was commander of the town's fort in the 1740s, ensuring that it was manned by militiamen, some of whom would have been gunners. In this print after a portrait by John Greenwood, Clarke wears an all-blue coat with brass buttons and a scarlet waistcoat edged with gold lace, and holds a telescope. The fort is shown in the background.

supply the 1st Battalion," 360 striped blankets and 145 camp kettles. Recruits in 1759 were issued "one good Coat, one pair of Buckskin Breeches, two Shirts, two pair of Stockings, two pair Shoes, and one Hat," but the uniform colors were not specified. They had muskets with bayonets and "Cartouch Boxes." (*A Narrative of the Military Actions of Colonel Marinus Willet*, New York, 1831; Brown University, Anne S.K. Brown Coll., Todd Albums; *New York Mercury*, March 5, 1759; PRO/WO 34/70)

G2: Officer, 2nd Connecticut Provincial Regiment, c.1758

The uniforms of Connecticut provincials were initially red. This figure is based on the portrait of Nathan Whiting (1724–71), lieutenant-colonel of the 2nd Regiment from 1755 and its colonel 1758–62, which shows a scarlet coat with yellow cuffs, lining and waistcoat, silver buttons and lace. Deserters from the 3rd Regiment in July 1759 had red coats "cuffed and lappeled with yellow." Blue coats with red lapels (and probably cuffs) were worn from 1760 by Connecticut provincials. Putnam's battalion raised in 1764 had no uniforms as "each man was to provide himself with suitable clothes." (Portrait attributed to John Durand at the Connecticut Historical Society, Hartford; *Connecticut Gazette*, July 7, 1759; *New London Summary*, June 13 &

July 11, 1760, and June 12, 1761; *Public Records of the Colony of Connecticut*, Hartford, 1881, XII)

G3: Private, Massachusetts Provincial Regiments, 1757–60

From February 1757, Massachusetts provincial soldiers were to have a blue cloth coat with red lapels and cuffs. Breeches could be blue or red, made of wool cloth, serge or drugget, or of buff leather. Waistcoats, when worn, could be blue, red or of other materials and, like stockings and shoes, seem often to have been civilian items. Once out in the field there were changes. Orders to Ruggle's Regiment at Fort Edward camp on June 21, 1759 stipulated that the "great hatts [tricorns] are [to be] cut so that the brims be 2 inches and a half wide and that no man wears a cap under his hat and more especially on duty." Gibson Clough of Bagley's Regiment recorded the following details regarding dress before leaving to garrison Fortress Louisbourg in 1759: April 18 "see that each man be equipped with a coat, waistcoat and breeches suitable for the campaign, also three good shirts, two good pairs of shoes, and two good pairs of stockings, and a hat..."; April 24, "...receive out of the stores ye defficiencies of gaiters and canteens, and powder horns [and] bullet pouches"; April 25, "...officers to see that their men have hats and to see that none wear trousers, none to wear caps when paraded..."; May 7, "sergeants and corporals of each company that they would provide themselves with blue coats and laced hats and the corporals to have yellow knots on their shoulders and ye drums green coats and also to use their utmost endeavors to persuade the privates their companies to get blue coats that there may be some uniform[ity] amongst the men and appear like soldiers. The commissary has a number of coats ready made... for ye privates..." Uniformity was rarer among the Massachusetts soldiers detached under Col.Frye at Fort Cumberland. On May 5, 1759, Capt.Knox noted that the "Privates are a poor, ragged set of men" and that "the ordinary soldiers had no uniforms nor do they affect any regularity." From April 1761 the three regiments raised had blue uniforms but the coats were now "faced and cuffed" with blue, red and green respectively. Hoar's Regiment had the "Blue Broad Cloth Coat, lapell'd & cuffed with red," but the facings are uncertain for Thwing's and Saltonstall's. Two deserters from Hoar's had blue regimentals with red lapels and cuffs (*Boston Gazette*, June 8, 1761; *Boston Post-Boy*, August 3, 1761). Two from Thwing's are described simply as wearing blue coats, which might imply that the regiment had all-blue coats (*Boston Gazette*, May 25, 1761; *Boston Post-Boy*, July 27, 1761). Deserters from Saltonstall's absconded wearing non-regimental blue or brown waistcoats or sailors' jackets. The men also had flannel waistcoats, "German serge" breeches, felt hats "bound with white ferret" lace and striped blankets (*Boston Weekly Newsletter*, February 25 & December 22 1757; Journal of Gibson Clough, 1759, Fortress Louisbourg National Historic Site; *Boston Post-Boy & Advertiser*, August 3, 1761; *Acts and Resolves... of... Massachusetts Bay*, Vols.15–17)

H1: Private, Boston Independent Company of Cadets, 1772

Only on April 22, 1772 at a meeting presided over by John Hancock, commander of the company and future signatory of the Declaration of Independence, was a uniform decided upon and described in detail. It consisted of a coat of "Scarle

Lieutenant Joshua Winslow (1727–1801), Massachusetts Militia, 1756. Scarlet coat and breeches, pale buff lapels, cuffs, lining and waistcoat, silver lace and buttons, silver-hilted sword with gold sword knot. (Print after J.S.Copley)

Broad Cloth with a narrow Round Cuff and a narrow Lapel of white Cloth, the Lapel to be the length of the waist of the Coat and a fall down Cape [collar] the Color of the Lapel, the Buttons to be plain white Mettle wash'd with silver, the Waistcoat and Breeches to be white with the same buttons." The hat was to be "small decorated with a large spangl'd Button and loop, Silver Loopings, a silver Band and Tossel, and common Cockades." The company had white linen "spadderdashes [gaiters] to be made to come up just over the knee and headed with a broad hem," to buckle with "a black garter below the knee, the Buttons to be black horn Small and placed at the exact distance of one inch from each other, the Buckles to be of white Mettall." The stock was white and worn with "a ruffled shirt the Wiggs and hair to be dressed at the sides club'd behind and well powder'd." A few days later on April 27, following the demands of the members of the company, the uniform was altered to "scarlet turned up with Buff instead of Scarlet and white." The style of uniform adopted was according to the British 1768 Clothing Warrant. (Coat in the Fort Ticonderoga Museum; H.C.McBarron, "Independent Company of Cadets, Massachusetts, 1772–1774," *MC&H*, II, December 1950, III, March 1951; uniform in the Fort Ticonderoga collection)

H2: Gunner, Independent Artillery Company of New London, Connecticut, 1762

While many colonial American artillery companies appear to have emulated the Royal Artillery's blue faced with scarlet, this company wore a blue "Broad Cloth" coat with buff cuffs and lapels, yellow metal buttons, a buff "jacket" (waistcoat), blue breeches, white stockings, and a black hat cockade; the men's hair was to be "Dressed with a wig or queue." (Order of March 8, 1762, Orderly Book, New London Historical Society, Document m.N.D.318; *New London Summary*, May 14, 1762)

H3: Officer, 11th New Hampshire Militia Regiment, 1774

The 11th Regiment was organized in late 1773 and gathered men from Concord (NH) and its immediate area. On January 15, 1774 the uniform of the regiment was decreed by the governor: "The officers to wear red coats, cuff'd, lin'd and lapel'd with sky-blue. Sky-blue waistcoats and breeches, all trim'd with white. Black hats with silver hat-band, button and loops, without lace. White stockings, cockade, sash and white [metal] gorgets. Swords with silver hilts. Captains and Lieutenants to carry fusees. Field officers to wear silver shoulder knots." (P.F.Copeland & J.P.Simpson, "11th New Hampshire Regiment 1774–1775," *MC&H*, XXI, Spring 1969)

INDEX

Figures in **bold** refer to illustrations